C-1143   CAREER EXAMINATION SERIES

*This is your
PASSBOOK for...*

Budget Analyst

*Test Preparation Study Guide
Questions & Answers*

COPYRIGHT NOTICE

This book is SOLELY intended for, is sold ONLY to, and its use is RESTRICTED to individual, bona fide applicants or candidates who qualify by virtue of having seriously filed applications for appropriate license, certificate, professional and/or promotional advancement, higher school matriculation, scholarship, or other legitimate requirements of education and/or governmental authorities.

This book is NOT intended for use, class instruction, tutoring, training, duplication, copying, reprinting, excerption, or adaptation, etc., by:

1) Other publishers
2) Proprietors and/or Instructors of "Coaching" and/or Preparatory Courses
3) Personnel and/or Training Divisions of commercial, industrial, and governmental organizations
4) Schools, colleges, or universities and/or their departments and staffs, including teachers and other personnel
5) Testing Agencies or Bureaus
6) Study groups which seek by the purchase of a single volume to copy and/or duplicate and/or adapt this material for use by the group as a whole without having purchased individual volumes for each of the members of the group
7) Et al.

Such persons would be in violation of appropriate Federal and State statutes.

PROVISION OF LICENSING AGREEMENTS – Recognized educational, commercial, industrial, and governmental institutions and organizations, and others legitimately engaged in educational pursuits, including training, testing, and measurement activities, may address request for a licensing agreement to the copyright owners, who will determine whether, and under what conditions, including fees and charges, the materials in this book may be used them. In other words, a licensing facility exists for the legitimate use of the material in this book on other than an individual basis. However, it is asseverated and affirmed here that the material in this book CANNOT be used without the receipt of the express permission of such a licensing agreement from the Publishers. Inquiries re licensing should be addressed to the company, attention rights and permissions department.

All rights reserved, including the right of reproduction in whole or in part, in any form or by any means, electronic or mechanical, including photocopying, recording, or by any information storage and retrieval system, without permission in writing from the Publisher.

Copyright © 2024 by
National Learning Corporation

212 Michael Drive, Syosset, NY 11791
(516) 921-8888 • www.passbooks.com
E-mail: info@passbooks.com

PASSBOOK® SERIES

THE *PASSBOOK® SERIES* has been created to prepare applicants and candidates for the ultimate academic battlefield – the examination room.

At some time in our lives, each and every one of us may be required to take an examination – for validation, matriculation, admission, qualification, registration, certification, or licensure.

Based on the assumption that every applicant or candidate has met the basic formal educational standards, has taken the required number of courses, and read the necessary texts, the *PASSBOOK® SERIES* furnishes the one special preparation which may assure passing with confidence, instead of failing with insecurity. Examination questions – together with answers – are furnished as the basic vehicle for study so that the mysteries of the examination and its compounding difficulties may be eliminated or diminished by a sure method.

This book is meant to help you pass your examination provided that you qualify and are serious in your objective.

The entire field is reviewed through the huge store of content information which is succinctly presented through a provocative and challenging approach – the question-and-answer method.

A climate of success is established by furnishing the correct answers at the end of each test.

You soon learn to recognize types of questions, forms of questions, and patterns of questioning. You may even begin to anticipate expected outcomes.

You perceive that many questions are repeated or adapted so that you can gain acute insights, which may enable you to score many sure points.

You learn how to confront new questions, or types of questions, and to attack them confidently and work out the correct answers.

You note objectives and emphases, and recognize pitfalls and dangers, so that you may make positive educational adjustments.

Moreover, you are kept fully informed in relation to new concepts, methods, practices, and directions in the field.

You discover that you are actually taking the examination all the time: you are preparing for the examination by "taking" an examination, not by reading extraneous and/or supererogatory textbooks.

In short, this PASSBOOK®, used directedly, should be an important factor in helping you to pass your test.

BUDGET ANALYST

DUTIES:
An employee in this class performs routine budget preparation and analysis in the preparation of budget requests for a large department or agency. Work is reviewed by a Senior Budget Analyst or department head through discussion, reports and observation of work in progress and upon completion. Does related work as required.

SCOPE OF THE EXAMINATION
The written test will cover knowledge, skills, and/or abilities in such areas as:
1. Budgeting;
2. Evaluating conclusions in lights of known facts;
3. Preparing written material;
4. Understanding and interpreting tabular material; and
5. Understanding and interpreting written material.

HOW TO TAKE A TEST

I. YOU MUST PASS AN EXAMINATION

A. *WHAT EVERY CANDIDATE SHOULD KNOW*

Examination applicants often ask us for help in preparing for the written test. What can I study in advance? What kinds of questions will be asked? How will the test be given? How will the papers be graded?

As an applicant for a civil service examination, you may be wondering about some of these things. Our purpose here is to suggest effective methods of advance study and to describe civil service examinations.

Your chances for success on this examination can be increased if you know how to prepare. Those "pre-examination jitters" can be reduced if you know what to expect. You can even experience an adventure in good citizenship if you know why civil service exams are given.

B. *WHY ARE CIVIL SERVICE EXAMINATIONS GIVEN?*

Civil service examinations are important to you in two ways. As a citizen, you want public jobs filled by employees who know how to do their work. As a job seeker, you want a fair chance to compete for that job on an equal footing with other candidates. The best-known means of accomplishing this two-fold goal is the competitive examination.

Exams are widely publicized throughout the nation. They may be administered for jobs in federal, state, city, municipal, town or village governments or agencies.

Any citizen may apply, with some limitations, such as the age or residence of applicants. Your experience and education may be reviewed to see whether you meet the requirements for the particular examination. When these requirements exist, they are reasonable and applied consistently to all applicants. Thus, a competitive examination may cause you some uneasiness now, but it is your privilege and safeguard.

C. *HOW ARE CIVIL SERVICE EXAMS DEVELOPED?*

Examinations are carefully written by trained technicians who are specialists in the field known as "psychological measurement," in consultation with recognized authorities in the field of work that the test will cover. These experts recommend the subject matter areas or skills to be tested; only those knowledges or skills important to your success on the job are included. The most reliable books and source materials available are used as references. Together, the experts and technicians judge the difficulty level of the questions.

Test technicians know how to phrase questions so that the problem is clearly stated. Their ethics do not permit "trick" or "catch" questions. Questions may have been tried out on sample groups, or subjected to statistical analysis, to determine their usefulness.

Written tests are often used in combination with performance tests, ratings of training and experience, and oral interviews. All of these measures combine to form the best-known means of finding the right person for the right job.

II. HOW TO PASS THE WRITTEN TEST

A. NATURE OF THE EXAMINATION

To prepare intelligently for civil service examinations, you should know how they differ from school examinations you have taken. In school you were assigned certain definite pages to read or subjects to cover. The examination questions were quite detailed and usually emphasized memory. Civil service exams, on the other hand, try to discover your present ability to perform the duties of a position, plus your potentiality to learn these duties. In other words, a civil service exam attempts to predict how successful you will be. Questions cover such a broad area that they cannot be as minute and detailed as school exam questions.

In the public service similar kinds of work, or positions, are grouped together in one "class." This process is known as *position-classification*. All the positions in a class are paid according to the salary range for that class. One class title covers all of these positions, and they are all tested by the same examination.

B. FOUR BASIC STEPS

1) Study the announcement

How, then, can you know what subjects to study? Our best answer is: "Learn as much as possible about the class of positions for which you've applied." The exam will test the knowledge, skills and abilities needed to do the work.

Your most valuable source of information about the position you want is the official exam announcement. This announcement lists the training and experience qualifications. Check these standards and apply only if you come reasonably close to meeting them.

The brief description of the position in the examination announcement offers some clues to the subjects which will be tested. Think about the job itself. Review the duties in your mind. Can you perform them, or are there some in which you are rusty? Fill in the blank spots in your preparation.

Many jurisdictions preview the written test in the exam announcement by including a section called "Knowledge and Abilities Required," "Scope of the Examination," or some similar heading. Here you will find out specifically what fields will be tested.

2) Review your own background

Once you learn in general what the position is all about, and what you need to know to do the work, ask yourself which subjects you already know fairly well and which need improvement. You may wonder whether to concentrate on improving your strong areas or on building some background in your fields of weakness. When the announcement has specified "some knowledge" or "considerable knowledge," or has used adjectives like "beginning principles of…" or "advanced … methods," you can get a clue as to the number and difficulty of questions to be asked in any given field. More questions, and hence broader coverage, would be included for those subjects which are more important in the work. Now weigh your strengths and weaknesses against the job requirements and prepare accordingly.

3) Determine the level of the position

Another way to tell how intensively you should prepare is to understand the level of the job for which you are applying. Is it the entering level? In other words, is this the position in which beginners in a field of work are hired? Or is it an intermediate or advanced level? Sometimes this is indicated by such words as "Junior" or "Senior" in the class title. Other jurisdictions use Roman numerals to designate the level – Clerk I, Clerk II, for example. The word "Supervisor" sometimes appears in the title. If the level is not indicated by the title, check the description of duties. Will you be working under very close supervision, or will you have responsibility for independent decisions in this work?

4) Choose appropriate study materials

Now that you know the subjects to be examined and the relative amount of each subject to be covered, you can choose suitable study materials. For beginning level jobs, or even advanced ones, if you have a pronounced weakness in some aspect of your training, read a modern, standard textbook in that field. Be sure it is up to date and has general coverage. Such books are normally available at your library, and the librarian will be glad to help you locate one. For entry-level positions, questions of appropriate difficulty are chosen -- neither highly advanced questions, nor those too simple. Such questions require careful thought but not advanced training.

If the position for which you are applying is technical or advanced, you will read more advanced, specialized material. If you are already familiar with the basic principles of your field, elementary textbooks would waste your time. Concentrate on advanced textbooks and technical periodicals. Think through the concepts and review difficult problems in your field.

These are all general sources. You can get more ideas on your own initiative, following these leads. For example, training manuals and publications of the government agency which employs workers in your field can be useful, particularly for technical and professional positions. A letter or visit to the government department involved may result in more specific study suggestions, and certainly will provide you with a more definite idea of the exact nature of the position you are seeking.

III. KINDS OF TESTS

Tests are used for purposes other than measuring knowledge and ability to perform specified duties. For some positions, it is equally important to test ability to make adjustments to new situations or to profit from training. In others, basic mental abilities not dependent on information are essential. Questions which test these things may not appear as pertinent to the duties of the position as those which test for knowledge and information. Yet they are often highly important parts of a fair examination. For very general questions, it is almost impossible to help you direct your study efforts. What we can do is to point out some of the more common of these general abilities needed in public service positions and describe some typical questions.

1) General information

Broad, general information has been found useful for predicting job success in some kinds of work. This is tested in a variety of ways, from vocabulary lists to questions about current events. Basic background in some field of work, such as sociology or economics, may be sampled in a group of questions. Often these are principles which have become familiar to most persons through exposure rather than through formal training. It is difficult to advise you how to study for these questions; being alert to the world around you is our best suggestion.

2) Verbal ability

An example of an ability needed in many positions is verbal or language ability. Verbal ability is, in brief, the ability to use and understand words. Vocabulary and grammar tests are typical measures of this ability. Reading comprehension or paragraph interpretation questions are common in many kinds of civil service tests. You are given a paragraph of written material and asked to find its central meaning.

3) Numerical ability

Number skills can be tested by the familiar arithmetic problem, by checking paired lists of numbers to see which are alike and which are different, or by interpreting charts and graphs. In the latter test, a graph may be printed in the test booklet which you are asked to use as the basis for answering questions.

4) Observation

A popular test for law-enforcement positions is the observation test. A picture is shown to you for several minutes, then taken away. Questions about the picture test your ability to observe both details and larger elements.

5) Following directions

In many positions in the public service, the employee must be able to carry out written instructions dependably and accurately. You may be given a chart with several columns, each column listing a variety of information. The questions require you to carry out directions involving the information given in the chart.

6) Skills and aptitudes

Performance tests effectively measure some manual skills and aptitudes. When the skill is one in which you are trained, such as typing or shorthand, you can practice. These tests are often very much like those given in business school or high school courses. For many of the other skills and aptitudes, however, no short-time preparation can be made. Skills and abilities natural to you or that you have developed throughout your lifetime are being tested.

Many of the general questions just described provide all the data needed to answer the questions and ask you to use your reasoning ability to find the answers. Your best preparation for these tests, as well as for tests of facts and ideas, is to be at your physical and mental best. You, no doubt, have your own methods of getting into an exam-taking mood and keeping "in shape." The next section lists some ideas on this subject.

IV. KINDS OF QUESTIONS

Only rarely is the "essay" question, which you answer in narrative form, used in civil service tests. Civil service tests are usually of the short-answer type. Full instructions for answering these questions will be given to you at the examination. But in case this is your first experience with short-answer questions and separate answer sheets, here is what you need to know:

1) Multiple-choice Questions

Most popular of the short-answer questions is the "multiple choice" or "best answer" question. It can be used, for example, to test for factual knowledge, ability to solve problems or judgment in meeting situations found at work.

A multiple-choice question is normally one of three types—
- It can begin with an incomplete statement followed by several possible endings. You are to find the one ending which *best* completes the statement, although some of the others may not be entirely wrong.
- It can also be a complete statement in the form of a question which is answered by choosing one of the statements listed.

- It can be in the form of a problem – again you select the best answer.

Here is an example of a multiple-choice question with a discussion which should give you some clues as to the method for choosing the right answer:

When an employee has a complaint about his assignment, the action which will *best* help him overcome his difficulty is to
   A. discuss his difficulty with his coworkers
   B. take the problem to the head of the organization
   C. take the problem to the person who gave him the assignment
   D. say nothing to anyone about his complaint

In answering this question, you should study each of the choices to find which is best. Consider choice "A" – Certainly an employee may discuss his complaint with fellow employees, but no change or improvement can result, and the complaint remains unresolved. Choice "B" is a poor choice since the head of the organization probably does not know what assignment you have been given, and taking your problem to him is known as "going over the head" of the supervisor. The supervisor, or person who made the assignment, is the person who can clarify it or correct any injustice. Choice "C" is, therefore, correct. To say nothing, as in choice "D," is unwise. Supervisors have and interest in knowing the problems employees are facing, and the employee is seeking a solution to his problem.

2) True/False Questions

The "true/false" or "right/wrong" form of question is sometimes used. Here a complete statement is given. Your job is to decide whether the statement is right or wrong.

SAMPLE: A roaming cell-phone call to a nearby city costs less than a non-roaming call to a distant city.

This statement is wrong, or false, since roaming calls are more expensive.

This is not a complete list of all possible question forms, although most of the others are variations of these common types. You will always get complete directions for answering questions. Be sure you understand *how* to mark your answers – ask questions until you do.

V. RECORDING YOUR ANSWERS

Computer terminals are used more and more today for many different kinds of exams.
For an examination with very few applicants, you may be told to record your answers in the test booklet itself. Separate answer sheets are much more common. If this separate answer sheet is to be scored by machine – and this is often the case – it is highly important that you mark your answers correctly in order to get credit.

An electronic scoring machine is often used in civil service offices because of the speed with which papers can be scored. Machine-scored answer sheets must be marked with a pencil, which will be given to you. This pencil has a high graphite content which responds to the electronic scoring machine. As a matter of fact, stray dots may register as answers, so do not let your pencil rest on the answer sheet while you are pondering the correct answer. Also, if your pencil lead breaks or is otherwise defective, ask for another.

Since the answer sheet will be dropped in a slot in the scoring machine, be careful not to bend the corners or get the paper crumpled.

The answer sheet normally has five vertical columns of numbers, with 30 numbers to a column. These numbers correspond to the question numbers in your test booklet. After each number, going across the page are four or five pairs of dotted lines. These short dotted lines have small letters or numbers above them. The first two pairs may also have a "T" or "F" above the letters. This indicates that the first two pairs only are to be used if the questions are of the true-false type. If the questions are multiple choice, disregard the "T" and "F" and pay attention only to the small letters or numbers.

Answer your questions in the manner of the sample that follows:

32. The largest city in the United States is
   A. Washington, D.C.
   B. New York City
   C. Chicago
   D. Detroit
   E. San Francisco

1) Choose the answer you think is best. (New York City is the largest, so "B" is correct.)
2) Find the row of dotted lines numbered the same as the question you are answering. (Find row number 32)
3) Find the pair of dotted lines corresponding to the answer. (Find the pair of lines under the mark "B.")
4) Make a solid black mark between the dotted lines.

VI. BEFORE THE TEST

Common sense will help you find procedures to follow to get ready for an examination. Too many of us, however, overlook these sensible measures. Indeed, nervousness and fatigue have been found to be the most serious reasons why applicants fail to do their best on civil service tests. Here is a list of reminders:

- Begin your preparation early – Don't wait until the last minute to go scurrying around for books and materials or to find out what the position is all about.
- Prepare continuously – An hour a night for a week is better than an all-night cram session. This has been definitely established. What is more, a night a week for a month will return better dividends than crowding your study into a shorter period of time.
- Locate the place of the exam – You have been sent a notice telling you when and where to report for the examination. If the location is in a different town or otherwise unfamiliar to you, it would be well to inquire the best route and learn something about the building.
- Relax the night before the test – Allow your mind to rest. Do not study at all that night. Plan some mild recreation or diversion; then go to bed early and get a good night's sleep.
- Get up early enough to make a leisurely trip to the place for the test – This way unforeseen events, traffic snarls, unfamiliar buildings, etc. will not upset you.
- Dress comfortably – A written test is not a fashion show. You will be known by number and not by name, so wear something comfortable.

- Leave excess paraphernalia at home – Shopping bags and odd bundles will get in your way. You need bring only the items mentioned in the official notice you received; usually everything you need is provided. Do not bring reference books to the exam. They will only confuse those last minutes and be taken away from you when in the test room.
- Arrive somewhat ahead of time – If because of transportation schedules you must get there very early, bring a newspaper or magazine to take your mind off yourself while waiting.
- Locate the examination room – When you have found the proper room, you will be directed to the seat or part of the room where you will sit. Sometimes you are given a sheet of instructions to read while you are waiting. Do not fill out any forms until you are told to do so; just read them and be prepared.
- Relax and prepare to listen to the instructions
- If you have any physical problem that may keep you from doing your best, be sure to tell the test administrator. If you are sick or in poor health, you really cannot do your best on the exam. You can come back and take the test some other time.

VII. AT THE TEST

The day of the test is here and you have the test booklet in your hand. The temptation to get going is very strong. Caution! There is more to success than knowing the right answers. You must know how to identify your papers and understand variations in the type of short-answer question used in this particular examination. Follow these suggestions for maximum results from your efforts:

1) Cooperate with the monitor

The test administrator has a duty to create a situation in which you can be as much at ease as possible. He will give instructions, tell you when to begin, check to see that you are marking your answer sheet correctly, and so on. He is not there to guard you, although he will see that your competitors do not take unfair advantage. He wants to help you do your best.

2) Listen to all instructions

Don't jump the gun! Wait until you understand all directions. In most civil service tests you get more time than you need to answer the questions. So don't be in a hurry. Read each word of instructions until you clearly understand the meaning. Study the examples, listen to all announcements and follow directions. Ask questions if you do not understand what to do.

3) Identify your papers

Civil service exams are usually identified by number only. You will be assigned a number; you must not put your name on your test papers. Be sure to copy your number correctly. Since more than one exam may be given, copy your exact examination title.

4) Plan your time

Unless you are told that a test is a "speed" or "rate of work" test, speed itself is usually not important. Time enough to answer all the questions will be provided, but this does not mean that you have all day. An overall time limit has been set. Divide the total time (in minutes) by the number of questions to determine the approximate time you have for each question.

5) Do not linger over difficult questions

If you come across a difficult question, mark it with a paper clip (useful to have along) and come back to it when you have been through the booklet. One caution if you do this – be sure to skip a number on your answer sheet as well. Check often to be sure that you have not lost your place and that you are marking in the row numbered the same as the question you are answering.

6) Read the questions

Be sure you know what the question asks! Many capable people are unsuccessful because they failed to *read* the questions correctly.

7) Answer all questions

Unless you have been instructed that a penalty will be deducted for incorrect answers, it is better to guess than to omit a question.

8) Speed tests

It is often better NOT to guess on speed tests. It has been found that on timed tests people are tempted to spend the last few seconds before time is called in marking answers at random – without even reading them – in the hope of picking up a few extra points. To discourage this practice, the instructions may warn you that your score will be "corrected" for guessing. That is, a penalty will be applied. The incorrect answers will be deducted from the correct ones, or some other penalty formula will be used.

9) Review your answers

If you finish before time is called, go back to the questions you guessed or omitted to give them further thought. Review other answers if you have time.

10) Return your test materials

If you are ready to leave before others have finished or time is called, take ALL your materials to the monitor and leave quietly. Never take any test material with you. The monitor can discover whose papers are not complete, and taking a test booklet may be grounds for disqualification.

VIII. EXAMINATION TECHNIQUES

1) Read the general instructions carefully. These are usually printed on the first page of the exam booklet. As a rule, these instructions refer to the timing of the examination; the fact that you should not start work until the signal and must stop work at a signal, etc. If there are any *special* instructions, such as a choice of questions to be answered, make sure that you note this instruction carefully.

2) When you are ready to start work on the examination, that is as soon as the signal has been given, read the instructions to each question booklet, underline any key words or phrases, such as *least, best, outline, describe* and the like. In this way you will tend to answer as requested rather than discover on reviewing your paper that you *listed without describing*, that you selected the *worst* choice rather than the *best* choice, etc.

3) If the examination is of the objective or multiple-choice type – that is, each question will also give a series of possible answers: A, B, C or D, and you are called upon to select the best answer and write the letter next to that answer on your answer paper – it is advisable to start answering each question in turn. There may be anywhere from 50 to 100 such questions in the three or four hours allotted and you can see how much time would be taken if you read through all the questions before beginning to answer any. Furthermore, if you come across a question or group of questions which you know would be difficult to answer, it would undoubtedly affect your handling of all the other questions.

4) If the examination is of the essay type and contains but a few questions, it is a moot point as to whether you should read all the questions before starting to answer any one. Of course, if you are given a choice – say five out of seven and the like – then it is essential to read all the questions so you can eliminate the two that are most difficult. If, however, you are asked to answer all the questions, there may be danger in trying to answer the easiest one first because you may find that you will spend too much time on it. The best technique is to answer the first question, then proceed to the second, etc.

5) Time your answers. Before the exam begins, write down the time it started, then add the time allowed for the examination and write down the time it must be completed, then divide the time available somewhat as follows:
   - If 3-1/2 hours are allowed, that would be 210 minutes. If you have 80 objective-type questions, that would be an average of 2-1/2 minutes per question. Allow yourself no more than 2 minutes per question, or a total of 160 minutes, which will permit about 50 minutes to review.
   - If for the time allotment of 210 minutes there are 7 essay questions to answer, that would average about 30 minutes a question. Give yourself only 25 minutes per question so that you have about 35 minutes to review.

6) The most important instruction is to *read each question* and make sure you know what is wanted. The second most important instruction is to *time yourself properly* so that you answer every question. The third most important instruction is to *answer every question*. Guess if you have to but include something for each question. Remember that you will receive no credit for a blank and will probably receive some credit if you write something in answer to an essay question. If you guess a letter – say "B" for a multiple-choice question – you may have guessed right. If you leave a blank as an answer to a multiple-choice question, the examiners may respect your feelings but it will not add a point to your score. Some exams may penalize you for wrong answers, so in such cases *only*, you may not want to guess unless you have some basis for your answer.

7) Suggestions
   a. Objective-type questions
      1. Examine the question booklet for proper sequence of pages and questions
      2. Read all instructions carefully
      3. Skip any question which seems too difficult; return to it after all other questions have been answered
      4. Apportion your time properly; do not spend too much time on any single question or group of questions

5. Note and underline key words – *all, most, fewest, least, best, worst, same, opposite,* etc.
6. Pay particular attention to negatives
7. Note unusual option, e.g., unduly long, short, complex, different or similar in content to the body of the question
8. Observe the use of "hedging" words – *probably, may, most likely,* etc.
9. Make sure that your answer is put next to the same number as the question
10. Do not second-guess unless you have good reason to believe the second answer is definitely more correct
11. Cross out original answer if you decide another answer is more accurate; do not erase until you are ready to hand your paper in
12. Answer all questions; guess unless instructed otherwise
13. Leave time for review

   b. Essay questions
     1. Read each question carefully
     2. Determine exactly what is wanted. Underline key words or phrases.
     3. Decide on outline or paragraph answer
     4. Include many different points and elements unless asked to develop any one or two points or elements
     5. Show impartiality by giving pros and cons unless directed to select one side only
     6. Make and write down any assumptions you find necessary to answer the questions
     7. Watch your English, grammar, punctuation and choice of words
     8. Time your answers; don't crowd material

8) Answering the essay question

Most essay questions can be answered by framing the specific response around several key words or ideas. Here are a few such key words or ideas:

M's: manpower, materials, methods, money, management
P's: purpose, program, policy, plan, procedure, practice, problems, pitfalls, personnel, public relations
   a. Six basic steps in handling problems:
     1. Preliminary plan and background development
     2. Collect information, data and facts
     3. Analyze and interpret information, data and facts
     4. Analyze and develop solutions as well as make recommendations
     5. Prepare report and sell recommendations
     6. Install recommendations and follow up effectiveness

   b. Pitfalls to avoid
     1. *Taking things for granted* – A statement of the situation does not necessarily imply that each of the elements is necessarily true; for example, a complaint may be invalid and biased so that all that can be taken for granted is that a complaint has been registered

2. *Considering only one side of a situation* – Wherever possible, indicate several alternatives and then point out the reasons you selected the best one
3. *Failing to indicate follow up* – Whenever your answer indicates action on your part, make certain that you will take proper follow-up action to see how successful your recommendations, procedures or actions turn out to be
4. *Taking too long in answering any single question* – Remember to time your answers properly

IX. AFTER THE TEST

Scoring procedures differ in detail among civil service jurisdictions although the general principles are the same. Whether the papers are hand-scored or graded by machine we have described, they are nearly always graded by number. That is, the person who marks the paper knows only the number – never the name – of the applicant. Not until all the papers have been graded will they be matched with names. If other tests, such as training and experience or oral interview ratings have been given, scores will be combined. Different parts of the examination usually have different weights. For example, the written test might count 60 percent of the final grade, and a rating of training and experience 40 percent. In many jurisdictions, veterans will have a certain number of points added to their grades.

After the final grade has been determined, the names are placed in grade order and an eligible list is established. There are various methods for resolving ties between those who get the same final grade – probably the most common is to place first the name of the person whose application was received first. Job offers are made from the eligible list in the order the names appear on it. You will be notified of your grade and your rank as soon as all these computations have been made. This will be done as rapidly as possible.

People who are found to meet the requirements in the announcement are called "eligibles." Their names are put on a list of eligible candidates. An eligible's chances of getting a job depend on how high he stands on this list and how fast agencies are filling jobs from the list.

When a job is to be filled from a list of eligibles, the agency asks for the names of people on the list of eligibles for that job. When the civil service commission receives this request, it sends to the agency the names of the three people highest on this list. Or, if the job to be filled has specialized requirements, the office sends the agency the names of the top three persons who meet these requirements from the general list.

The appointing officer makes a choice from among the three people whose names were sent to him. If the selected person accepts the appointment, the names of the others are put back on the list to be considered for future openings.

That is the rule in hiring from all kinds of eligible lists, whether they are for typist, carpenter, chemist, or something else. For every vacancy, the appointing officer has his choice of any one of the top three eligibles on the list. This explains why the person whose name is on top of the list sometimes does not get an appointment when some of the persons lower on the list do. If the appointing officer chooses the second or third eligible, the No. 1 eligible does not get a job at once, but stays on the list until he is appointed or the list is terminated.

X. HOW TO PASS THE INTERVIEW TEST

The examination for which you applied requires an oral interview test. You have already taken the written test and you are now being called for the interview test – the final part of the formal examination.

You may think that it is not possible to prepare for an interview test and that there are no procedures to follow during an interview. Our purpose is to point out some things you can do in advance that will help you and some good rules to follow and pitfalls to avoid while you are being interviewed.

What is an interview supposed to test?

The written examination is designed to test the technical knowledge and competence of the candidate; the oral is designed to evaluate intangible qualities, not readily measured otherwise, and to establish a list showing the relative fitness of each candidate – as measured against his competitors – for the position sought. Scoring is not on the basis of "right" and "wrong," but on a sliding scale of values ranging from "not passable" to "outstanding." As a matter of fact, it is possible to achieve a relatively low score without a single "incorrect" answer because of evident weakness in the qualities being measured.

Occasionally, an examination may consist entirely of an oral test – either an individual or a group oral. In such cases, information is sought concerning the technical knowledges and abilities of the candidate, since there has been no written examination for this purpose. More commonly, however, an oral test is used to supplement a written examination.

Who conducts interviews?

The composition of oral boards varies among different jurisdictions. In nearly all, a representative of the personnel department serves as chairman. One of the members of the board may be a representative of the department in which the candidate would work. In some cases, "outside experts" are used, and, frequently, a businessman or some other representative of the general public is asked to serve. Labor and management or other special groups may be represented. The aim is to secure the services of experts in the appropriate field.

However the board is composed, it is a good idea (and not at all improper or unethical) to ascertain in advance of the interview who the members are and what groups they represent. When you are introduced to them, you will have some idea of their backgrounds and interests, and at least you will not stutter and stammer over their names.

What should be done before the interview?

While knowledge about the board members is useful and takes some of the surprise element out of the interview, there is other preparation which is more substantive. It *is* possible to prepare for an oral interview – in several ways:

1) Keep a copy of your application and review it carefully before the interview

This may be the only document before the oral board, and the starting point of the interview. Know what education and experience you have listed there, and the sequence and dates of all of it. Sometimes the board will ask you to review the highlights of your experience for them; you should not have to hem and haw doing it.

2) Study the class specification and the examination announcement

Usually, the oral board has one or both of these to guide them. The qualities, characteristics or knowledges required by the position sought are stated in these documents. They offer valuable clues as to the nature of the oral interview. For example, if the job involves supervisory responsibilities, the announcement will usually indicate that knowledge of modern supervisory methods and the qualifications of the candidate as a supervisor will be tested. If so, you can expect such questions, frequently in the form of a hypothetical situation which you are expected to solve. NEVER go into an oral without knowledge of the duties and responsibilities of the job you seek.

3) Think through each qualification required

Try to visualize the kind of questions you would ask if you were a board member. How well could you answer them? Try especially to appraise your own knowledge and background in each area, *measured against the job sought*, and identify any areas in which you are weak. Be critical and realistic – do not flatter yourself.

4) Do some general reading in areas in which you feel you may be weak

For example, if the job involves supervision and your past experience has NOT, some general reading in supervisory methods and practices, particularly in the field of human relations, might be useful. Do NOT study agency procedures or detailed manuals. The oral board will be testing your understanding and capacity, not your memory.

5) Get a good night's sleep and watch your general health and mental attitude

You will want a clear head at the interview. Take care of a cold or any other minor ailment, and of course, no hangovers.

What should be done on the day of the interview?

Now comes the day of the interview itself. Give yourself plenty of time to get there. Plan to arrive somewhat ahead of the scheduled time, particularly if your appointment is in the fore part of the day. If a previous candidate fails to appear, the board might be ready for you a bit early. By early afternoon an oral board is almost invariably behind schedule if there are many candidates, and you may have to wait. Take along a book or magazine to read, or your application to review, but leave any extraneous material in the waiting room when you go in for your interview. In any event, relax and compose yourself.

The matter of dress is important. The board is forming impressions about you – from your experience, your manners, your attitude, and your appearance. Give your personal appearance careful attention. Dress your best, but not your flashiest. Choose conservative, appropriate clothing, and be sure it is immaculate. This is a business interview, and your appearance should indicate that you regard it as such. Besides, being well groomed and properly dressed will help boost your confidence.

Sooner or later, someone will call your name and escort you into the interview room. *This is it.* From here on you are on your own. It is too late for any more preparation. But remember, you asked for this opportunity to prove your fitness, and you are here because your request was granted.

What happens when you go in?

The usual sequence of events will be as follows: The clerk (who is often the board stenographer) will introduce you to the chairman of the oral board, who will introduce you to the other members of the board. Acknowledge the introductions before you sit down. Do not be surprised if you find a microphone facing you or a stenotypist sitting by. Oral interviews are usually recorded in the event of an appeal or other review.

Usually the chairman of the board will open the interview by reviewing the highlights of your education and work experience from your application – primarily for the benefit of the other members of the board, as well as to get the material into the record. Do not interrupt or comment unless there is an error or significant misinterpretation; if that is the case, do not hesitate. But do not quibble about insignificant matters. Also, he will usually ask you some question about your education, experience or your present job – partly to get you to start talking and to establish the interviewing "rapport." He may start the actual questioning, or turn it over to one of the other members. Frequently, each member undertakes the questioning on a particular area, one in which he is perhaps most competent, so you can expect each member to participate in the examination. Because time is limited, you may also expect some rather abrupt switches in the direction the questioning takes, so do not be upset by it. Normally, a board member will not pursue a single line of questioning unless he discovers a particular strength or weakness.

After each member has participated, the chairman will usually ask whether any member has any further questions, then will ask you if you have anything you wish to add. Unless you are expecting this question, it may floor you. Worse, it may start you off on an extended, extemporaneous speech. The board is not usually seeking more information. The question is principally to offer you a last opportunity to present further qualifications or to indicate that you have nothing to add. So, if you feel that a significant qualification or characteristic has been overlooked, it is proper to point it out in a sentence or so. Do not compliment the board on the thoroughness of their examination -- they have been sketchy, and you know it. If you wish, merely say, "No thank you, I have nothing further to add." This is a point where you can "talk yourself out" of a good impression or fail to present an important bit of information. Remember, *you close the interview yourself.*

The chairman will then say, "That is all, Mr. _____, thank you." Do not be startled; the interview is over, and quicker than you think. Thank him, gather your belongings and take your leave. Save your sigh of relief for the other side of the door.

How to put your best foot forward

Throughout this entire process, you may feel that the board individually and collectively is trying to pierce your defenses, seek out your hidden weaknesses and embarrass and confuse you. Actually, this is not true. They are obliged to make an appraisal of your qualifications for the job you are seeking, and they want to see you in your best light. Remember, they must interview all candidates and a non-cooperative candidate may become a failure in spite of their best efforts to bring out his qualifications. Here are 15 suggestions that will help you:

1) Be natural – Keep your attitude confident, not cocky

If you are not confident that you can do the job, do not expect the board to be. Do not apologize for your weaknesses, try to bring out your strong points. The board is interested in a positive, not negative, presentation. Cockiness will antagonize any board member and make him wonder if you are covering up a weakness by a false show of strength.

2) Get comfortable, but don't lounge or sprawl

Sit erectly but not stiffly. A careless posture may lead the board to conclude that you are careless in other things, or at least that you are not impressed by the importance of the occasion. Either conclusion is natural, even if incorrect. Do not fuss with your clothing, a pencil or an ashtray. Your hands may occasionally be useful to emphasize a point; do not let them become a point of distraction.

3) Do not wisecrack or make small talk

This is a serious situation, and your attitude should show that you consider it as such. Further, the time of the board is limited – they do not want to waste it, and neither should you.

4) Do not exaggerate your experience or abilities

In the first place, from information in the application or other interviews and sources, the board may know more about you than you think. Secondly, you probably will not get away with it. An experienced board is rather adept at spotting such a situation, so do not take the chance.

5) If you know a board member, do not make a point of it, yet do not hide it

Certainly you are not fooling him, and probably not the other members of the board. Do not try to take advantage of your acquaintanceship – it will probably do you little good.

6) Do not dominate the interview

Let the board do that. They will give you the clues – do not assume that you have to do all the talking. Realize that the board has a number of questions to ask you, and do not try to take up all the interview time by showing off your extensive knowledge of the answer to the first one.

7) Be attentive

You only have 20 minutes or so, and you should keep your attention at its sharpest throughout. When a member is addressing a problem or question to you, give him your undivided attention. Address your reply principally to him, but do not exclude the other board members.

8) Do not interrupt

A board member may be stating a problem for you to analyze. He will ask you a question when the time comes. Let him state the problem, and wait for the question.

9) Make sure you understand the question

Do not try to answer until you are sure what the question is. If it is not clear, restate it in your own words or ask the board member to clarify it for you. However, do not haggle about minor elements.

10) Reply promptly but not hastily

A common entry on oral board rating sheets is "candidate responded readily," or "candidate hesitated in replies." Respond as promptly and quickly as you can, but do not jump to a hasty, ill-considered answer.

11) Do not be peremptory in your answers

A brief answer is proper – but do not fire your answer back. That is a losing game from your point of view. The board member can probably ask questions much faster than you can answer them.

12) Do not try to create the answer you think the board member wants

He is interested in what kind of mind you have and how it works – not in playing games. Furthermore, he can usually spot this practice and will actually grade you down on it.

13) Do not switch sides in your reply merely to agree with a board member

Frequently, a member will take a contrary position merely to draw you out and to see if you are willing and able to defend your point of view. Do not start a debate, yet do not surrender a good position. If a position is worth taking, it is worth defending.

14) Do not be afraid to admit an error in judgment if you are shown to be wrong

The board knows that you are forced to reply without any opportunity for careful consideration. Your answer may be demonstrably wrong. If so, admit it and get on with the interview.

15) Do not dwell at length on your present job

The opening question may relate to your present assignment. Answer the question but do not go into an extended discussion. You are being examined for a *new* job, not your present one. As a matter of fact, try to phrase ALL your answers in terms of the job for which you are being examined.

Basis of Rating

Probably you will forget most of these "do's" and "don'ts" when you walk into the oral interview room. Even remembering them all will not ensure you a passing grade. Perhaps you did not have the qualifications in the first place. But remembering them will help you to put your best foot forward, without treading on the toes of the board members.

Rumor and popular opinion to the contrary notwithstanding, an oral board wants you to make the best appearance possible. They know you are under pressure – but they also want to see how you respond to it as a guide to what your reaction would be under the pressures of the job you seek. They will be influenced by the degree of poise you display, the personal traits you show and the manner in which you respond.

ABOUT THIS BOOK

This book contains tests divided into Examination Sections. Go through each test, answering every question in the margin. We have also attached a sample answer sheet at the back of the book that can be removed and used. At the end of each test look at the answer key and check your answers. On the ones you got wrong, look at the right answer choice and learn. Do not fill in the answers first. Do not memorize the questions and answers, but understand the answer and principles involved. On your test, the questions will likely be different from the samples. Questions are changed and new ones added. If you understand these past questions you should have success with any changes that arise. Tests may consist of several types of questions. We have additional books on each subject should more study be advisable or necessary for you. Finally, the more you study, the better prepared you will be. This book is intended to be the last thing you study before you walk into the examination room. Prior study of relevant texts is also recommended. NLC publishes some of these in our Fundamental Series. Knowledge and good sense are important factors in passing your exam. Good luck also helps. So now study this Passbook, absorb the material contained within and take that knowledge into the examination. Then do your best to pass that exam.

EXAMINATION SECTION

EXAMINATION SECTION
TEST 1

DIRECTIONS: Each question or incomplete statement is followed by several suggested answers or completions. Select the one that BEST answers the question or completes the statement. *PRINT THE LETTER OF THE CORRECT ANSWER IN THE SPACE AT THE RIGHT.*

1. Constitutional limitations on borrowing by local governments are less relevant today than 20 to 30 years ago PRIMARILY because of the

    A. continually rising rate of interest on mortgages
    B. growing importance of local non-property taxes
    C. growth in federal aid
    D. more rapid growth of the suburbs relative to central cities

2. Assume that the manager of an office or administrative activity has been cautioned to control the cost of peak load fluctuations and unforeseen emergencies in preparing his budget estimates.
    In conforming to these instructions, the manager should NOT budget for

    A. a reserve of trained employees
    B. *floating* or traveling trouble-shooting employees
    C. overtime work
    D. part-time help

3. A mail section consisted of incoming and outgoing units. By applying an hourly work count, a supervisor found that the peak load of the incoming unit occurred in the morning and almost equalled the peak load of the outgoing unit in the afternoon. As a result, the two units were combined. The former condition is BEST described as an example of

    A. decentralization   B. overspecialization
    C. overstaffing   D. reorganization

4. Of the following, the one whose yield would be MOST difficult to predict in preparing a budget is the _____ tax.

    A. commercial rent or occupancy   B. general corporation
    C. sales   D. transportation corporation

5. Of the following, the MOST useful data to use in predicting the yield of the sales tax normally are

    A. corporate profits
    B. personal incomes
    C. the deflated gross national product
    D. unemployment rates

6. Of the following, the criterion that is LEAST desirable for the selection of an output indicator for use in multi-year program analysis is

    A. cost effectiveness   B. data availability
    C. relevance   D. simplicity

7. The MOST valid generalization regarding the attribute as a form of data is that it is

   A. a source of contamination in the analysis of the basic problem
   B. distinguishable from other forms of data in varying amounts
   C. relatively impervious to scientific treatment because of its subjectivity
   D. a quality, trait, or function that is present or absent

8. The one of the following management techniques that would generally be LEAST useful in the work of a budget examiner is a _____ system.

   A. management information
   B. network type planning and scheduling
   C. paperwork simplification
   D. work measurement

9. A supervisor thought it necessary to maintain a double check for accuracy on the review of cases. A work count showed him that Reviewer A found a percentage of errors of 12 percent, whereas Reviewer B, spending the same amount of time, turned up an additional 0.1 percent of errors. Of the following, it would be MOST advisable for the supervisor to

   A. commend the first reviewer and discipline the second reviewer
   B. divide the percentage of errors equally between the two
   C. eliminate a second review in the future
   D. reclassify the first reviewer

10. Of the following, the one that BEST describes a well-defined economic criterion for assigning priorities to feasible projects is

    A. unit pricing theory
    B. diminishing marginal utility
    C. discounted cash flow rate of return
    D. economies of scale

11. The technical research term *stanine* refers to a(n)

    A. economical approximation for validity
    B. regressed form of the true score
    C. reliable measure of physical fitness
    D. special form of the standard score

12. A score NOT based upon the standard deviation is the

    A. scaled score
    B. T-score
    C. z-score
    D. percentile rank

13. PPBS is MOST difficult to apply to problems of

    A. fire   B. health   C. public works   D. welfare

14. Which of the following types of problems would be LEAST likely to lend itself to *operations research?*

    A. Determining program priorities
    B. Developing a controlled backlog
    C. Distribution of resources and jobs
    D. Sequence of work

15. The MOST valid of the following statements regarding measurement of government activities is:

    A. A viable program cannot be planned without work measurement
    B. Most government activities cannot be measured
    C. Some aspects of every activity can be measured
    D. Work measurement takes more time and effort than it is worth

    15.____

16. In correlating results on reading and intelligence tests for a given set of population, the BEST data to utilize are

    A. intelligence quotient and reading quotient
    B. mental age and reading age
    C. mental age and reading grade
    D. raw scores on both tests

    16.____

17. For the purpose of conducting a school survey, the practice of selecting a typical county on the basis of considerable known information about all of the counties in the United States is an example of _____ sampling.

    A. purposive   B. representative
    C. nested   D. cluster

    17.____

18. Which one of the following problems is generally NOT encountered in cost analysis of multi-year plans for an ongoing program?

    A. Form in which costs should be summarized for decision-making
    B. Magnitude of uncertainty in cost estimates
    C. The obtaining of historical costs
    D. The question of price level changes

    18.____

19. Select the statement which is MOST valid:

    A. Accounting object classes should be the categories of a program structure
    B. Each program should be related to the operations of a single agency
    C. The costs for each program should form the basis of the accounting system
    D. The costs for each program should include the costs of all relevant object classes

    19.____

20. Assume that the number of buses (U_t) required for a given line-haul system serving the Central Business District depends upon roundtrip time (t), capacity of bus (c), and the total number of people to be moved in a peak hour (P) in the major direction, i.e., in the morning and out in the evening.
    The formula for the number of buses required is: $U_t =$

    A. Ptc   B. $\frac{tp}{c}$ C. $\frac{cp}{t}$ D. $\frac{ct}{p}$

    20.____

21. The area, in blocks, that can be served by a single stop for any maximum walking distance is given by the following formula: $a = 2w^2$. In this formula, a = the area served by a stop, and w = maximum walking distance.
    If people will tolerate a walk of up to three blocks, how many stops would be needed to service an area of 288 square blocks?

    A. 9   B. 16   C. 18   D. 27

    21.____

22. Among the following, the MOST appropriate technique for ascertaining the content of educational achievement is

    A. the analysis of textbooks and courses of study
    B. the reliance on the judgment of experts
    C. differential achievement by varied grades
    D. statistical correlations with class marks

23. Which of the following is a network chart? _____ chart.

    A. Critical path method   B. Gantt
    C. Multi-column process   D. Single-column process

24. Such measures as cost of square foot per road are MOST useful for

    A. evaluating goal attainment
    B. evaluation of current operations
    C. manning tables
    D. output plans

Questions 25-28.

DIRECTIONS: Questions 25 through 28 are to be answered on the basis of the following paragraph.

Under institutional training program 1, two-thirds of the recipients are poor, 40 percent are under 21 years of age, and the average net earnings gained by the participants are almost three times the per trainee cost. A competing program 2 increases the average earnings by only 120 percent of the per trainee cost but all participants are poor and under 21.

25. If the sole objective of the governmental agency is the greatest return to national income per dollar invested, the PREFERABLE alternative is

    A. 1   B. either 1 or 2
    C. 2   D. a combination of 1 and 2

26. If the basic objective is to assist youth, the PREFERABLE alternative is

    A. 1   B. either 1 or 2
    C. 2   D. a combination of 1 and 2

27. If the basic objective is to assist the poor, the PREFERABLE alternative is

    A. 1   B. either 1 or 2
    C. 2   D. a combination of 1 and 2

28. If the objectives are multiple: assist youth, assist the poor, and the greatest return to national income per dollar invested, the choice of the PREFERABLE program

    A. cannot be made
    B. is 1
    C. is 2
    D. depends on an appropriate weighting of objectives

29. ACIR refers to Advisory Commission on

    A. Industrial Resources
    B. Intergovernmental Relations
    C. Internal Revenue
    D. Institutional Research

30. The Constitution of the United States

    A. does not mention the budget process
    B. provides for an executive budget
    C. mandates a national budget, but does not specify procedure
    D. specifies the basic steps of budget preparation and authorization

31. The following four steps represent an analysis of an experimental procedure:
    I. Collection of evidence
    II. Appraisal of the tentative generalization
    III. Adoption of the operational hypotheses
    IV. Definition of problem
    The steps should be taken in the following order:

    A. III, IV, I, II
    B. I, II, III, IV
    C. IV, III, I, II
    D. II, I, IV, III

Questions 32-34.

DIRECTIONS: Questions 32 through 34 are to be answered on the basis of the following data.

A series of cost-benefit studies of various alternative health programs yields the following results:

Program	Benefit	Cost
K	30	15
L	60	60
M	300	150
N	600	500

In answering Questions 32 through 34, assume that all programs can be increased or decreased in scale without affecting their individual benefit-to-cost ratios.

32. The benefit-to-cost ratio of Program M is

    A. 10:1   B. 5:1   C. 2:1   D. 1:2

33. The budget ceiling for one or more of the programs included in the study is set at 75 units.
    It may MOST logically be concluded that

    A. Programs K and L should be chosen to fit within the budget ceiling
    B. Program K would be the most desirable one that could be afforded
    C. Program M should be chosen rather than Program K
    D. the choice should be between Program M and K

34. If no assumptions can be made regarding the effects of change of scale, the MOST logical conclusion, on the basis of the data available, is that

    A. more data are needed for a budget choice of program
    B. Program K is the most preferable because of its low cost and good benefit-to-cost ratio
    C. Program M is the most preferable because of its high benefits and good benefit-to-cost ratio
    D. there is no difference between Programs K and M, and either can be chosen for any purpose

35. The PRIMARY obstacle to the interpretation of educational experiments in which two or more groups of students have been matched on chronological age or intelligence is:

    A. Significance tests are not adequate to handle the data
    B. The matching process frequently inflates group differences
    C. Chronological age and intelligence are usually the wrong variables on which to equate students
    D. Populations of matched students do not exist to which to generalize

36. The LARGEST item of expenditure in the typical office or administrative organization is usually for

    A. charges for office machine usage
    B. office supplies, forms, and other materials
    C. rent of space occupied
    D. salaries and wages

37. Of the following, the MOST appropriate indicator of quality of service in a health program is usually

    A. average daily in-patient load in a general hospital
    B. number of children served in a disease-screening clinic
    C. number of patients treated in an alcoholic clinic
    D. number of therapy hours of care provided in a mental hospital

Questions 38-47.

DIRECTIONS: Questions 38 through 47 consists of a quotation which contains one word that is incorrectly used because it is not in keeping with the meaning that the quotation is evidently intended to convey. Determine which word is INCORRECTLY used. Then, select from the words lettered A, B, C, or D the word which, when substituted for the incorrectly used word, would BEST help to convey the meaning of the quotation.

38. A measure must be developed of all direct and indirect benefits, recognizing the non-quantifiable nature of many of the latter, yet guarding against the tendency to use the quantifiable as a justification for any difference between costs and benefits.

    A. cannot   B. non-quantifiable
    C. effects   D. ability

39. A persistent problem in the rationalization of public expenditures in the natural resources field stems from the varied objectives of different interests. A primary reason for this is that the cost and gains of contemplated actions are perceived clearly.

    A. differently
    B. minor
    C. potential
    D. programs

40. It is not imperative that the agency's table of organization follow the program structure rigidly, but a general parallelism is helpful, both in placing legislative responsibility for goal attainment and in program evaluation.

    A. executive
    B. harmful
    C. ineffective
    D. initiative

41. Some of the impediments to developing appropriate data systems stem from the fact that organization lines and program structures do not expand. The requirement for accounting on a program basis is superimposed across organizational requirements.

    A. coincide
    B. conflict
    C. inducements
    D. planning

42. Examples of a public good may be found also in domestic programs, although national income is probably the purest and most extreme example of a public good.

    A. international
    B. least
    C. private
    D. security

43. To avoid distortions in cost-benefit calculations, an appropriate discount interest rate should be calculated on the basis of the marginal cost principle.

    A. analysis
    B. estimated
    C. opportunity
    D. time horizon

44. Where budget deficits are developed at the agency level for use by operating bureaus, they must be harmonious with the directives that have come from the central budget office.

    A. assumptions
    B. consistent
    C. departmental
    D. large

45. A possible source of budgetary waste could be eliminated if estimates were prepared in no greater detail than was justified by their magnitude.

    A. accuracy
    B. budgets
    C. complexity
    D. mechanical

46. A capital budget may provide information useful in estimating national income. This is a very different type of consideration from budgetary and policy-formulation purposes.

    A. contain
    B. economic
    C. program
    D. wealth

47. In some governments, the failure to bring budgeting and policy-making together at the operating level is often unfortunately attributable to the presence of a strong budget office attached to the chief executive, which is too concerned with threats to its authority.

    A. departmental
    B. effectiveness
    C. involved
    D. planning

48. The MOST important function served by a line-item budget is to

   A. control appropriations and expenditures in detail
   B. give the Budget Bureau information on each operating agency's financial plans
   C. measure cost-effectiveness
   D. provide a basis for management analysis

49. Assume that work to be distributed varies in difficulty and complexity. The workers are at junior and senior levels and differ in competence within each level.
Of the following, the BEST policy for the supervisor to follow in this case when distributing work is usually to

   A. divide the work among workers based on the individual speed and competence of each worker, regardless of worker level
   B. give the more difficult work to the seniors, and base the number of work units given to each level on the estimated time needed to complete each different work unit
   C. give the more difficult work to the seniors and the less difficult to the juniors, but give more units of work to the juniors
   D. give the work which will require the longest time to complete to the seniors

50. Generally, authority and responsibility for an activity should NOT be delegated until

   A. all authorized positions have been filled
   B. an organization is mature
   C. personnel have been trained in the staff functions
   D. policies can be spelled out so as to insure uniform administration

KEY (CORRECT ANSWERS)

1.	B	11.	D	21.	B	31.	C	41.	A
2.	A	12.	D	22.	A	32.	C	42.	D
3.	B	13.	D	23.	A	33.	D	43.	C
4.	B	14.	A	24.	B	34.	A	44.	A
5.	B	15.	C	25.	A	35.	D	45.	A
6.	A	16.	D	26.	C	36.	D	46.	D
7.	D	17.	A	27.	C	37.	D	47.	A
8.	C	18.	C	28.	D	38.	B	48.	A
9.	C	19.	D	29.	B	39.	A	49.	B
10.	C	20.	B	30.	A	40.	A	50.	D

TEST 2

DIRECTIONS: Each question or incomplete statement is followed by several suggested answers or completions. Select the one that BEST answers the question or completes the statement. *PRINT THE LETTER OF THE CORRECT ANSWER IN THE SPACE AT THE RIGHT.*

Questions 1-7.

DIRECTIONS: Questions 1 through 7 are to be answered on the basis of the following paragraphs. Indicate the correct answer for these questions as follows: If the paragraphs indicate it is true, mark answer A. If the paragraphs indicate it is probably true, mark answer B. If the paragraphs indicate it is probably false, mark answer C. If the paragraphs indicate it is false, mark answer D.

The fallacy underlying what some might call the eighteenth and nineteenth century misconceptions of the nature of scientific investigations seems to lie in a mistaken analogy. Those who said they were investigating the structure of the universe imagined themselves as the equivalent of the early explorers and mapmakers. The explorers of the fifteenth and sixteenth centuries had opened up new worlds with the aid of imperfect maps; in their accounts of distant lands, there had been some false and many ambiguous statements. But by the time everyone came to believe the world was round, the maps of distant continents were beginning to assume a fairly consistent pattern. By the seventeenth century, methods of measuring space and time had laid the foundations for an accurate geography.

On this basic issue, there is far from complete agreement among philosophers of science today. You can, each of you, choose your side and find highly distinguished advocates for the point of view you have selected. However, in view of the revolution in physics, anyone who now asserts that science is an exploration of the universe must be prepared to shoulder a heavy burden of proof. To my mind, the analogy between the mapmaker and the scientist is false. A scientific theory is not even the first approximation to a map; it is not a need; it is a policy -- an economical and fruitful guide to action, by scientific investigators.

1. The author thinks that 18th and 19th century science followed the same technique as the 15th century geographers.   1._____

2. The author disagrees with the philosophers who are labelled realists.   2._____

3. The author believes there is a permanent structure to the universe.   3._____

4. A scientific theory is an economical guide to exploring what cannot be known absolutely.   4._____

5. Philosophers of science accept the relativity implications of recent research in physics.   5._____

6. It is a matter of time and effort before modern scientists will be as successful as the geographers.   6._____

7. The author believes in an indeterminate universe.   7._____

8. Total government expenditures, Federal, State, and local, are APPROXIMATELY the following proportion of Gross National Product: 8._____

    A. 1/10   B. 1/5   C. 1/3   D. 1/2

Questions 9-12.

DIRECTIONS: Questions 9 through 12 are to be answered on the basis of the following.

The income elasticity of demand for selected items of consumer demand in the United States are:

Item	Elasticity
Airline travel	5.66
Alcohol	.62
Dentist fees	1.00
Electric utilities	3.00
Gasoline	1.29
Intercity bus	1.89
Local bus	1.41
Restaurant meals	.75

9. The demand for the item listed below that would be MOST adversely affected by a decrease in income is

   A. alcohol
   B. electric utilities
   C. gasoline
   D. restaurant meals

10. The item whose relative change in demand would be the same as the relative change in income would be

    A. dentist fees
    B. gasoline
    C. restaurant meals
    D. none of the above

11. If income increases by 12 percent, the demand for restaurant meals may be expected to increase by

    A. 9 percent
    B. 12 percent
    C. 16 percent
    D. none of the above

12. On the basis of the above information, the item whose demand would be MOST adversely affected by an increase in the sales tax from 7 percent to 8 percent to be passed on to the consumer in the form of higher prices

    A. would be airline travel
    B. would be alcohol
    C. would be gasoline
    D. cannot be determined

13. The PRIMARY purpose of randomization principles in the design of experiments is to

    A. exclude a number of alternative interpretations
    B. objectify the experimental evidence
    C. validate the tests of significance
    D. equate the number of degrees of freedom in the cells

14. Of the following, the GREATEST advantage of state collection as against local collection of local sales taxes in the state is:

A. Payments by retailers to the tax agency may be made at less frequent intervals
B. The burden of the tax is decreased
C. The net yield of the tax is increased
D. The tax rate is uniform throughout the state

15. A criticism of a *pay-as-you-go* policy in financing capital outlay is that it

    A. is more costly
    B. is more difficult to administer
    C. may be difficult to determine priorities among projects
    D. may lead to the postponement of needed projects

16. Which of the following tends to be the LEAST constraint encountered in the preparation of a municipal budget?

    A. Legislative   B. Political
    C. Revenue   D. Personnel

17. In the last two decades, the ability of the legislature to review the budget has been improved in many governments PRINCIPALLY by providing

    A. a long-range planning system
    B. for public hearings on the budget
    C. more details in the executive budget
    D. professional staff for the legislature

18. Recent research shows that some lower-level professional employees feel that they accomplish little in their work that is worthwhile.
    Management experts usually say that the one of the following which BEST explains such feelings is

    A. dissatisfaction among employees provoked by the activities of labor unions
    B. frequent salary increases unmatched by any significant increases in productivity
    C. the almost total indifference of employees to the vital issues of the times
    D. the failure to properly develop in these employees an understanding of the significance of their work

19. One way to get maximum effort from employees is for management to give employees the maximum possible personal freedom in accomplishing agency objectives.
    This encourages a feeling of self-management which is MOST basic to

    A. an impartial approach to work
    B. tightly coordinated team effort
    C. high levels of motivation
    D. uniformity of action

20. Interactions among public programs are often complex. The situation that is NOT an example of such interactions is:

    A. A solid waste disposal program may increase air pollution
    B. Changes in transportation may improve or reduce retail trade
    C. Paving of more highway mileage may enlarge traffic congestion
    D. Traffic control systems may reduce or enlarge motor vehicle accidents

21. The following are given as the objectives of a department's mission: 21.____
    I. Economic efficiency
    II. Optimal use of environmental resources
    III. Safety
    IV. Support of other national interests
    Which one of the departments listed below is MOST likely to have all four of the above objectives?

    A. Correction   B. Education
    C. Health   D. Transportation

22. An agency is considering the hiring of a consultant for a given project. 22.____
    Of the following, the GREATEST danger of reliance on outside experts is:

    A. It delays the work program because of the necessity of processing bids
    B. It does not contribute to internal staff capacity
    C. It involves greater project costs
    D. The resulting work, though excellent, may not be assimilated in the governmental process

23. Of the following, the MOST pertinent argument given against *revenue-sharing* is: 23.____

    A. Local governments are incapable of planning expenditures properly
    B. The expenditure needs of state and local governments have not grown as rapidly as the needs of the federal government
    C. The federal government has the more lucrative sources of revenue at its disposal
    D. There would be no flow-through to cities

24. In fixing beneficiary charges, governments generally do NOT consider 24.____

    A. the cost of the service
    B. the rate of return
    C. the value of the service
    D. what the market will bear

25. The MAXIMUM amount of the real property tax levy does NOT usually depend upon the 25.____

    A. assessed valuation
    B. equalization rate
    C. size of the budget
    D. value of tax-exempt property

26. An argument against the use of a task force for budget analysis is: 26.____
    It could

    A. facilitate participation of the agencies concerned
    B. not help clarify problems of coordination
    C. not result in in-depth considerations
    D. overemphasize subject matter areas singled out for intensive effort

27. A standard cost system produces 27.____

   A. a ratio of cost of goods sold to net sales
   B. a ratio of current assets to current liabilities
   C. original actual costs which may be compared to inflated costs
   D. predetermined costs which can be compared with actual costs

28. Which of the following is NOT a desirable characteristic of a capital budget? 28.____

   A. A long-range capital improvements plan (6 years)
   B. A master plan for physical development of the city (10-25 years)
   C. Financial analysis of present and anticipated municipal revenue
   D. Omission of operating expenses and other recurrent costs

29. The earmarking of revenues is often defended since it 29.____

   A. improves tax administration
   B. is a non-political device
   C. provides a direct link between the cost and benefit of a service
   D. simplifies the budgetary process

30. Of the following, the BEST measure of relative taxable capacity among states is 30.____

   A. per capita personal income
   B. per capita yield of a stock transfer tax
   C. personal income
   D. the yield of a sales tax

31. In identifying fundamental government objectives under PPBS, the LEAST important of the following questions is 31.____

   A. By whom is it to be done?
   B. For whom is it to be done?
   C. What is to be done?
   D. Why is each activity currently performed being done?

32. Which one of the following measures is of LEAST use as an output measure for a PPBS system? 32.____

   A. Gallons of water per housing unit
   B. Number of days of hospital care per capita
   C. Number of traffic accidents by 1,000 vehicle miles
   D. Number of traffic tickets per officer

33. Estimates of costs can be MOST *rough* for which of the following purposes? 33.____

   A. Budget
   B. One-year program and financial plan
   C. Program analyses
   D. Quarterly allotment system

34. A city built a golf course on land that it owns. In this situation, 34.____

   A. no additional costs are involved
   B. the cost is the initial cost of the land

C. the cost is related to possible alternate uses of the land
D. the cost is the initial cost adjusted for price changes

35. Two ten-year programs are estimated to have the same cost. Alternative 1 involves high costs in the early years and lower costs later. Alternative 2 incurs lowest costs initially and higher costs later.
In this case,

   A. Alternative 1 has the higher present discounted cost
   B. Alternative 2 has the higher present discounted cost
   C. the alternative with the higher present discounted cost cannot be determined from the information given
   D. both alternatives have exactly the same present discounted cost

35.____

36. Governmental accounting should serve as a tool of management.
This statement refers to the design of an accounting system to do which one of the following?

   A. Maintain accounts that permit an independent audit extending to all records, funds, securities, and property.
   B. Make possible a determination of the adequacy of custodianship of government assets by responsible officials.
   C. Make possible the measurements of activities at the administrative unit level.
   D. Show compliance with legal provisions.

36.____

37. Budgetary reform in the United States during the first quarter of the twentieth century emphasized control over the administrative agencies and _____ budgeting.

   A. accrual   B. executive
   C. legislative   D. program

37.____

38. The one basis of budgetary appropriation that is almost universally used is

   A. capital   B. economic character
   C. performance unit   D. organizational unit

38.____

39. The LEAST useful of the following bases of budgetary classification for a municipality would generally be by

   A. economic character   B. object-item of expetur
   C. organizational unit D. program or activity

39.____

40. A functional classification of municipal budgetary expenditures is USUALLY prepared because it

   A. helps remove the budget from the political arena
   B. is required by local law
   C. keeps the public informed about the nature of governmental operations
   D. minimizes unnecessary budgetary appropriations

40.____

41. The following equation is used to estimate operating expenditures of a city: $Y = 90.2 + 6.2X$, where Y = operating expenditures in millions of dollars and where X = years.
Origin: Fiscal year 1989-90.
The equation indicates that operating expenditures may be expected to

41.____

A. level off at $96.4 million
B. increase at a rate of 6.2 percent per year
C. increase by $6.2 million per year
D. increase by $90.2 million per year

42. Of the following concepts associated with PPBS, the one that MOST distinguishes it from the basic characteristics of all prior forms of budgeting is 42.____

    A. input
    B. output
    C. systems analysis
    D. time span of budget appropriation

43. Of the following categories, the one which would receive the GREATEST percentage of total funds in a city executive capital budget would MOST LIKELY be for 43.____

    A. education   B. environmental protection
    C. health services   D. public safety

44. Among the sub-programs of a Physical and Mental Well-Being Program, a sub-program, Unassignable Items, is indicated. Unassignable items MOST likely would include 44.____

    A. Drug Addiction Treatment
    B. Mental Illness Prevention
    C. Physical Health
    D. Research and Planning

45. Under a PPBS system, it is BEST to account for employee benefit costs 45.____

    A. by applying them to individual programs
    B. by omitting them from relevant costs
    C. in a separate category
    D. in a special overhead account

46. In preparing the budget of expenses for any office or administrative unit, some expenses originate in and are chargeable directly to the office or administrative unit. Others must be allocated on some basis.
    Of the following, the expense that is LEAST typical of a direct expense, and therefore should be charged on an allocated basis, is 46.____

    A. depreciation of machines and equipment
    B. employee fringe benefits and salaries
    C. printing expense
    D. rent

47. Justification materials generally found in conventional budgets have failings as analysis documents because they 47.____

    A. do not contain comparisons with prior year budgets
    B. seldom discuss alternatives sufficiently
    C. very rarely contain work-load data
    D. very rarely provide information

48. Post-completion audits of capital expense projects are made for a variety of purposes. Of the following, the LEAST appropriate purpose for such an audit is to

   A. aid in assessing future capital expenditures proposals
   B. assess the abilities and competence of the analyst who submitted the original project proposal
   C. reveal reasons for project failures
   D. verify the resulting savings

49. The one of the following kinds of problems for which administrative measuring techniques tend to be LEAST applicable is

   A. administrative planning
   B. decisions in the realm of human relations
   C. determining relative effectiveness of alternative procedures and methods
   D. work programming

50. The one of the following which is an example of transfer payments by government is

   A. intergovernmental aid
   B. late payments of encumbered balances
   C. social security payments
   D. transportation payments for government employees

KEY (CORRECT ANSWERS)

1. D	11. A	21. D	31. A	41. C
2. B	12. D	22. D	32. D	42. C
3. D	13. C	23. A	33. C	43. A
4. A	14. C	24. B	34. C	44. D
5. D	15. D	25. C	35. A	45. A
6. D	16. D	26. D	36. C	46. D
7. B	17. D	27. D	37. B	47. B
8. C	18. D	28. C	38. D	48. B
9. B	19. C	29. C	39. A	49. B
10. A	20. B	30. A	40. C	50. C

EXAMINATION SECTION
TEST 1

DIRECTIONS: Each question or incomplete statement is followed by several suggested answers or completions. Select the one that BEST answers the question or completes the statement. *PRINT THE LETTER OF THE CORRECT ANSWER IN THE SPACE AT THE RIGHT.*

1. Among the following, the MOST regressive tax is the _____ tax.

    A. sales   B. gasoline   C. entertainment   D. hotel

2. When a suburban community has a high proportion of industrial/commercial property, its real estate tax rate is likely to be relatively

    A. *high*, primarily because of load put on community facilities by the added traffic
    B. *low*, primarily because its school taxes will be low
    C. *high*, primarily because business and industry demand special services
    D. *low*, primarily because business and especially industrial areas need little police and fire protection at night and such costs are less at that time

3. A fare increase in a public transport system usually produces a less than proportionate increase in revenues PRIMARILY because of

    A. wasteful operations
    B. reduced economy of scale
    C. price elasticity of demand
    D. dishonesty by operating personnel

4. A larger sewage disposal system costs less per unit of capacity than the same system in a smaller area.
   This characteristic is known as

    A. reduced cost-benefit ratio   B. economy of scale
    C. diseconomy of scale   D. vertical integration

5. Assume that inflation has caused an increase in the average income of residents of a city which has a progressive income tax system. Assume also that there is no change in the relevant laws.
   As a result, the effect on tax revenues

    A. is proportional to the increase in personal income
    B. is proportionately smaller than the increase in personal income
    C. is proportionately greater than the increase in personal income
    D. cannot be determined without further information

6. The timing and valuation of benefits is the distinguishing feature of which of the following?

    A. Job evaluation   B. Program budgeting
    C. Planning-programming-budgeting   D. Operations forecasting

17

7. The planning technique for complex projects which focuses on the scheduling, timing, and sequencing of their individual operations is MOST appropriately called

   A. PERT B. PPBS C. MIS D. EOQ Model

8. Before a PPB system can function, there has to be a specification of

   A. procedures
   B. methods
   C. costs and benefits
   D. goals

9. In the budgeting process, the FIRST major aim of the planning portion is the

   A. estimate of total revenues
   B. detailed itemization of inputs
   C. detailed itemization of outputs
   D. quantification of the program's outputs

10. In addition to quantifying the desired results and costs of programs, PPB also considers as MOST important their

    A. political desirability
    B. timing
    C. management
    D. public image

11. In governmental budgeting, the area in which benefits can be measured MOST easily is

    A. education
    B. defense spending
    C. any area in which the same product or service is obtainable commercially
    D. any area in which the agency concerned has had really long experience

12. Among government services meant for ultimate consumption, the supply of city water as compared to its price

    A. has strong price elasticity with respect to demand
    B. is essentially inelastic in demand with respect to price
    C. has negative price elasticity of demand
    D. varies at random with respect to price elasticity

13. In economic analysis, the cost of time used for anything is

    A. the value of the best alternative use of the same time
    B. determined by wage costs in union contracts
    C. set arbitrarily
    D. determined by historical trends subjected to statistical analysis

14. In determining the amount of detail which should be included in a public announcement of a new budgetary program, it is generally CORRECT that

    A. all known details should be included
    B. there is an optimal amount of detail for the effect the announcement is designed to obtain
    C. the maximum amount of detail is given so as to reduce the program's vulnerability to criticism
    D. there are so many uncertainties that any standard should not even be established

15. In the process of approving a new budget, opportunities to explain questioned budget items are offered FIRST to the

    A. chief fiscal officer of the city
    B. mayor's office, for items other than its own budget
    C. agency head involved
    D. appropriate committee of the city council

16. The PRINCIPAL objective of budgetary control is to

    A. see that an agency carries out its authorized functions within the limits of funds available
    B. minimize the expenditures of money by specific agencies
    C. place limitations on money expended for specific activities
    D. exercise line supervision over purchasing and payroll functions

17. Computers are MOST useful in budgeting in

    A. providing the basic data
    B. making decisions
    C. doing analytical operations on the data
    D. quantifying qualitative data

18. As understood by the budgeter, a model of a program is a(the)

    A. survey of its feasibility
    B. description of the relationship between inputs and outputs
    C. survey related to performance evaluation
    D. first stage of its implementation

19. With respect to private and public facilities of the same kind, the CHIEF accounting differences between the two operations lie in the areas of taxes, profits, and

    A. depreciation   B. internal auditing
    C. disbursements   D. receipts

20. In the absence of other information, the value of government service output is measured in national income accounts

    A. at cost of inputs
    B. at cost of inputs plus an allowance for extra benefits
    C. at cost of inputs minus an allowance for excess cost
    D. by estimates independent of costs

21. Strong seasonal variation in local industry is MOST clearly reflected in receipts for _____ tax.

    A. city income   B. sales
    C. franchise   D. business property

22. A government agency decides to decentralize its functions. Assuming that this process can be accomplished without new construction, i.e., in existing offices, the agency's budget will

    A. *decrease,* chiefly because decentralization always cuts red tape
    B. *increase,* chiefly because decentralization usually means duplicating at least some activities
    C. *decrease,* chiefly because some functions become unnecessary
    D. *increase,* chiefly because there is greater chance for empire building

22.____

23. Performance budgeting is MOST closely related to which of the following techniques for describing an approach to management?

    A. The managerial grid
    B. Management by exception
    C. Management by objectives
    D. Operations research

23.____

24. In cost-benefit analysis, certain non-tangible factors are given implicit values. The MOST common implicit estimate, of the ones listed below, defines the value of

    A. political feasibility
    B. sunk costs
    C. a human life
    D. aesthetics

24.____

25. Labor productivity among non-supervising employees, in man-hours per unit of output, is MOST easily measured in a(n)

    A. municipal asphalt plant
    B. department of sanitation truck repair shop
    C. income tax audit section
    D. engineering design office

25.____

26. Of the following, the BEST definition of *full funding* of a budget item is

    A. arranging for the commitment of funds from state and federal agencies
    B. funding the total cost, including indirect charges
    C. preparing a special bond issue
    D. putting the whole cost into the first year's budget of the agency

26.____

27. As contrasted to the traditional line-item budget, PPBS

    A. makes long-range planning easier
    B. facilitates very detailed review by the legislative branch
    C. makes larger projects more difficult to control than others
    D. reduces cost overruns in capital projects

27.____

28. To provide funds to support a legally balanced budget, the city sometimes relies on

    A. general obligation bonds
    B. tax anticipation notes
    C. special agency obligations
    D. deferring bill payments

28.____

29. The KEY to any attempt to prevent setbacks in governmental programs is to

    A. provide an adequate budget
    B. give proper consideration to long-run and short-run needs

29.____

C. concentrate managerial attention on short-run problems
D. reduce environmental limitations

30. The one of the following options which gives the MOST complete accounting of the factors upon which expenditure estimates by budget analysts are usually based is administrative

    A. units
    B. units and work programs
    C. units, work programs, and physical units required
    D. units, work programs, physical inputs required, and an estimate of social costs

31. The one of the following areas in which past expenditures are usually NOT used as a basis for estimating future expenditures is in

    A. reordering supplies and operation of office machinery
    B. replacement of office machinery
    C. payment of telephone bills
    D. maintenance of roads

32. Historically, *performance budgeting* was

    A. synonymous with line-item budgeting
    B. synonymous with PPBS
    C. an intermediate stage before PPBS
    D. superseded by line-item budgeting

33. The development of performance budgets are characterized by the use of a particular technique called

    A. computer analysts
    B. time and motion study
    C. efficiency rating of personnel
    D. cost effectiveness analysis

34. Of the following, which is generally considered to be the PRINCIPAL advantage of lump-sum appropriations?

    A. Legislatures need be given little detail of expenditures.
    B. Public hearings on the budget are greatly simplified.
    C. Pressures toward efficiency in an agency are reduced.
    D. Agency heads have more flexibility in internal operations.

35. City expense and capital budgets are prepared separately because

    A. expense budgets can be prepared for a year at a time whereas capital budgets deal only with long-range expenses
    B. expense budgets must be met from current revenues whereas capital budgets are met from borrowings
    C. common elements make it convenient to do so
    D. the expense budget depends on internal auditing practices whereas the capital budget is not affected

36. The MOST difficult part of budget review is a decision about 36.____

    A. recruitment of staff
    B. the importance of the program under review
    C. possible cost savings through elimination of certain jobs in the program
    D. the size of the proposed appropriation

37. The RELATIVE worth of alternative budgetary items may be judged in terms of _____ 37.____
    cost(s).

    A. sunk   B. opportunity
    C. unavoidable   D. out-of-pocket

38. The creation of maximum efficiency within an agency without regard to costs incurred 38.____
    elsewhere is termed

    A. system optimization   B. maximization
    C. micro-economic analysis D. suboptimization

39. The term *full system cost* in governmental programs is taken to mean all direct and indi- 39.____
    rect

    A. costs incurred by the city in the project
    B. government costs at all levels
    C. public and private costs
    D. public and private costs as well as opportunity

40. Budget control is concerned MAINLY with 40.____

    A. making sure agencies do their job
    B. the formulation of tax policy
    C. the enforcement of tax collections
    D. measures to ensure honesty in governmental disbursements

41. The standard of management performance which the comptroller is expected to enforce 41.____
    is essentially that of

    A. making sure all the money is spent
    B. adequate record keeping
    C. operational efficiency
    D. ensuring that legal authorization exists for agency expenditures

42. *Comprehensive budgeting* is synonymous with 42.____

    A. full-system budgeting   B. zero-base budgeting
    C. incremental budgeting   D. cost-benefit analysis

43. *Systems analysis* impinges on the budget process MAINLY by 43.____

    A. reducing the need for budgetary review
    B. setting up systems and procedures for doing the job
    C. increasing the need for budgetary review
    D. requiring a large computer installation

44. Programs of federal assistance to state and local governments are HARD for budgetary authorities to evaluate because   44.____

    A. *assisting* is hard to define in terms of results
    B. the level of such assistance is nearly always inadequate
    C. federal and state contributions are highly restrictive
    D. responsibility for results is not clearly delineated

45. In the PERT project planning method, slack time is the difference between   45.____

    A. the most likely estimated time and the maximum
    B. minimum and maximum estimated time along the critical path
    C. the critical time and the expected time
    D. time along the critical path and another path

46. The PERT planning method is MUCH facilitated by   46.____

    A. computer execution
    B. special peripheral equipment, notably x-y plotters
    C. the theory of waiting lines
    D. Monte Carlo methods

47. Management by exception is facilitated by which one of the following managerial methods?   47.____

    A. Theory X
    B. Theory Y
    C. Fixed systems and procedures
    D. The managerial grid

48. In the PERT project planning method, the critical path is the   48.____

    A. maximum elapsed time to completion
    B. maximum average elapsed time to completion
    C. maximum expected elapsed time to completion
    D. best method of doing the job

49. Zero-base budgeting cannot be used universally PRIMARILY because   49.____

    A. it is too time-consuming to do properly
    B. there are mandatory programs which must be funded
    C. it reduces the efficient functioning of the agency whose budget is concerned
    D. the information for doing it is not always available

50. In establishing standards for clerical or physical tasks, it is MOST appropriate to use a(the)   50.____

    A. theoretical value
    B. absolute value, based on current study
    C. expected value and an expression of variability
    D. expected value and a time trend pertaining to it

KEY (CORRECT ANSWERS)

1. A	11. C	21. B	31. B	41. D
2. B	12. B	22. B	32. C	42. B
3. C	13. A	23. C	33. D	43. B
4. B	14. B	24. C	34. D	44. D
5. C	15. C	25. A	35. B	45. D
6. C	16. A	26. D	36. B	46. A
7. A	17. C	27. A	37. B	47. C
8. D	18. B	28. B	38. D	48. C
9. A	19. A	29. B	39. D	49. B
10. B	20. A	30. C	40. A	50. C

TEST 2

DIRECTIONS: Each question or incomplete statement is followed by several suggested answers or completions. Select the one that BEST answers the question or completes the statement. *PRINT THE LETTER OF THE CORRECT ANSWER IN THE SPACE AT THE RIGHT.*

1. All modern governments have developed specific procedures to ensure accountability for the receipt and expenditure of public funds. The steps in one such procedure are given below, out of their logical order.
   Select the option which BEST presents these stages in their logical sequence.
   I. Disbursing officers provide for the payment of cash or check to satisfy the liability.
   II. The central financial authority (treasury) places money at the disposal of disbursing officers.
   III. The heads of agencies extend to designated officials within the agency the authorization to incur obligations. Designated officials award contracts for goods and services and incur obligations for the payment of salaries.
   IV. The legislature authorizes the chief executive to make expenditure authority available to administrative agencies. The executive authority responsible for the execution of the budget, in accordance with legislative action, extends to the agencies authorization to incur obligations.
   V. Fiscal officers within agencies prepare and certify vouchers to show that obligations are due and payable by disbursing officers. Orders for payment are prepared by fiscal officers and submitted to disbursing officers.

   The BEST logical sequence is:

   A. II, V, IV, I, III B. III, II, V, I, IV
   C. IV, III, II, V, I D. V, I, III, IV, II

   1.____

2. In a complex organization, particularly one with field offices, where generally similar activities are conducted in more than one location and administered by different organizational units, agency budgeting can be MOST facilitated by the use of which one of the following techniques?

   A. Gantt charting   B. Factorial estimating
   C. Econometric models   D. Double budgeting

   2.____

Questions 3-5.

DIRECTIONS: Each of Questions 3 through 5 consists of a paragraph which contains one word that is incorrectly used because it is NOT in keeping with the meaning that the paragraph is evidently intended to convey. Determine which word is incorrectly used. Select from the choices lettered A, B, C, and D the word which, when substituted for the incorrectly used word, would BEST help to convey the meaning of the paragraph.

3. More difficult to set are standards not expressed in either physical or monetary measurements. What standard can a budget examiner use for determining the competence of an attorney or a personnel officer? What can he use for determining whether the agency's recruiting program meets both short- and long-term objectives? Or whether the public relations program is successful? Are supervisors loyal to the agency's objectives? Such questions show how difficult it is to establish standards for goals that cannot be given clear quantitative or qualitative measurement. Many definite standards exist in agencies because thorough research into what constitutes desired performance has not been done above the level of the repair shop, the stockroom, or the accounting department. Perhaps a more important reason is that where human relationships count in performance, it is very hard to measure what is *good, effective,* or *efficient.*

   A. completely
   B. meaningless
   C. resist
   D. reinforcement

4. The fact that some programs are not subject to constant budgetary review and that government budgets thus come to be at least partially uncontrollable has been viewed with great concern by some authorities. There is no doubt that strongly entrenched programs sustain the overall effectiveness of budgetary review. But in these circumstances, *uncontrollable* is probably a misnomer. These outlays can be controlled, but they may be irreducible. In many cases, programs are so well established, so strongly supported by interest groups, and so much a part of accepted public policy that frequent and searching budgetary review, extending to annual examination of substantive legislation, would be somewhat pointless. If there is widespread agreement, inside and outside the legislature, that veterans should receive pensions for service-connected disabilities, there is no need for extensive hearings before appropriations committees on the merits of funds for veterans' pensions.
   A change in policy toward veterans is not likely to come from appropriations committees.

   A. premature
   B. overriding
   C. misdirected
   D. limit

5. Promptness is a great virtue in control reports. Unfortunately, it is often difficult to be both prompt and accurate. An accurate evaluation may require a certain amount of investigation and double-checking. The person making an evaluation naturally wants to be sure he can justify his conclusions. In addition, delay is likely to be compounded if a report is prepared by someone who is trained to balance accounts to the last penny. A hospital administrator, for example, was having great difficulty in keeping down expenses partly because expense reports did not become available until six to eight weeks following the events presumably being controlled. Executives who use control reports should be fully aware of what kind of information they are getting. If they insist on prompt reports, they must learn to disregard substantial variations and to expect some false alarms. On the other hand, if they are interested in having the full facts and being deliberate in taking action, then they need a different kind of report. Because most organizations need both accurate and timely reports, managerial skill is required to ensure that the control reports are really suited to their purposes.

   A. annul
   B. insignificant
   C. monitoring
   D. unequivocal

6. Historically, those who favor *legislative* rather than executive budgeting assert that legislative budgeting would

   A. result in a better separation of powers
   B. cut down government spending
   C. be less susceptible to special pressure groups
   D. produce balanced budgets

7. In 2012, a department bought a piece of a certain supply item for a total of $x. In 2013, the department bought k percent fewer of the item but had to pay a total of g percent more for it.
   Which of the following formulae is CORRECT for determining the average price per item in 2013?

   A. $100\dfrac{xg}{nk}$
   B. $\dfrac{x(100+g)}{n(100-k)}$
   C. $\dfrac{x(100-g)}{n(100+k)}$
   D. $\dfrac{x}{n} - 100\dfrac{g}{k}$

8. A sample of 18 income tax returns, each with 4 personal exemptions, is taken for 2011 and for 2012. The breakdown is as follows in terms of income:

Average gross income (in thousands)	Number of returns 2011	Number of returns 2012
4	6	2
8	10	11
12	2	5

   There is a personal deduction per exemption of $500. There are no other expense deductions. In addition, there is an exclusion of $3000 for incomes less than $5000 and $2000 for incomes from $5000 to $9999.99. From $10,000 upward, there is no exclusion. Total net taxable income for the samples (in thousands) for 2011 is MOST NEARLY

   A. $60   B. $85   C. $10   D. $128

9. In the preceding question, the increase in total net taxable income for the sample (in thousands) between 2011 and 2012 is

   A. 18   B. 20   C. 24   D. 34

Questions 10-12.

DIRECTIONS: Answer Questions 10 through 12 on the basis of the following information.

Four batches of lightbulbs purchased by the city from four different suppliers contained defective units in the following percentages:

Supplier	Number	Percent Defective
A	3,000	1.2
B	5,000	1.4
C	4,000	1.6
D	8,000	0.8

10. The COMBINED percent defective is

   A. 1.25   B. 1.21   C. 1.17   D. 1.10

11. A further 13,000 bulbs split proportionately among the suppliers would have a number defective of about

   A. 152   B. 162   C. 175   D. 330

12. A systematic comparison of the quality of the four suppliers' products is called

   A. operations research
   B. cost-effectiveness analysis
   C. cost-benefit analysis
   D. value analysis

Questions 13-15.

DIRECTIONS: Answer Questions 13 through 15 on the basis of the following information.

In 2014, a police precinct records 456 oases of car thefts which is 22.6 percent of all grand larcenies. In 2015, there were 560 such cases, which constituted 35% of the broader category.

13. The number of crimes in the broader category in 2015 was MOST NEARLY

   A. 1600   B. 1700   C. 1960   D. 2800

14. The change from 2014 to 2015 in the number of crimes in the broader category represented MOST NEARLY a

   A. 2.5% decrease
   B. 10.1% increase
   C. 12.5% increase
   D. 20% decrease

15. In 2015, one out of every 6 of these crimes was solved. This represents MOST NEARLY what percentage of the total number of crimes in the broader category that year?

   A. 5.8   B. 6   C. 9.3   D. 12

16. Assume that a maintenance shop does 5 brake jobs to every 3 front-end jobs. It does 8000 jobs altogether in a 240-day year. In one day, one worker can do 3 front-end jobs or 4 brake jobs.
    About how many workers will be needed in the shop?

   A. 3   B. 5   C. 10   D. 18

17. Assume that the price of a certain item declines by 6 percent one year and then increases by 5 and 10 percent, respectively, during the next two years.
    What is the OVERALL increase in price over the three-year period?

   A. 4.2   B. 6   C. 8.6   D. 10.1

18. After finding the total percent change in a price (TC) over a three-year period, as in the preceding question, one could compute the average annual percent change in the price by using the formula:

A. $(1+TC)^{1/3}$ B. $\dfrac{(1+TC)}{3}$

C. $(1+TC)^{1/3}-1$ D. $\dfrac{1}{(1+TC)\sqrt[3]{3-1}}$

Questions 19-21.

DIRECTIONS: Answer Questions 19 through 21 on the basis of the following information.

The number of applications processed per day by a group of clerks can be expressed as follows:

Characteristic	No. Processed Per Day
mean	34.6
median	29.6
minimum	18.3
maximum	47.7

19. On the basis of the information given, it would be WRONG to conclude that

    A. the data are normally distributed
    B. the data are skewed to the right
    C. a suitable histogram could have a lower limit of 15 and an upper limit of 49.9
    D. employees processed more than 29.6 applications each per day

20. The range is

    A. 14.7   B. 29.4   C. 33.0   D. 66.0

21. The mid-range is

    A. 14.7   B. 29.4   C. 33.0   D. 66.0

Questions 22-25.

DIRECTIONS: Questions 22 through 25 are to be answered on the basis of the following information.

Assume that the Department of Industrial Waste and Combustibles of the City of Silver Keys is trying to decide what fee it will oharge private engineering organizations for a specific type of laboratory analysis that it performs for them. The Department's laboratory is equipped to process as many as 250 waste and soot samples per day. The Commissioner of Industrial Waste and Combustibles knows that at $5 per analysis, the laboratory will operate to capacity. He is convinced that raising the price will cause the private engineering organizations to perform the analyses themselves rather than submit their samples to the laboratory. On the average, he expects to lose one sample for each 2.5 cent increase in the fee (Chart A). The Commissioner's cost data indicate that there is a fixed expense of $275 to run the laboratory for one day. Extra technicians, supplies, and so forth, add a variable cost of $3 per sample for each sample analyzed.

CHART A

Fee	Number of Analyses	Income
$5.00	250	$1250.00
5.25	240	1260.00
5.50	230	1265.00
5.75	220	1265.00
6.00	210	1260.00
6.25	200	1250.00
6.50	190	1235.00
6.75	180	1215.00
7.00	170	1190.00
7.25	160	1160.00
7.50	150	1125.00
7.75	140	1085.00

22. Each five-cent rise in the fee will

   A. *decrease* expenses by $60
   B. *decrease* expenses by $30
   C. *increase* expenses by $12
   D. *decrease* expenses by $6

23. According to Chart A, if the Department sets its fee at a level that brings in the maximum net income, the number of samples it would receive will be MOST NEARLY

   A. 165 B. 188 C. 205 D. 215

24. Which of the following conclusions can LOGICALLY be drawn from the above information?

   A. Eventually, the decrease in the number of samples submitted for analysis will not be offset by the increase in the fee.
   B. Each time the fee is raised, net income will increase.
   C. Net income will increase until the total expense equals the fixed expense plus the variable expense; thereafter, net income will remain constant.
   D. Maximum gross returns will be reached each time the fee is raised.

25. For the Department to obtain maximum net income, the fee should be set between

   A. $7.50 and $7.75
   B. $7.00 and $7.25
   C. $6.25 and $6.50
   D. $5.25 and $5.75

26. Assume that supervisor S has four subordinates - A, B, C, and D.
    The MAXIMUM number of relationships, assuming that all combinations are included, that can exist between S and his subordinates is

   A. 28 B. 15 C. 7 D. 4

27. If the workmen's compensation insurance rate for clerical workers is 93 cents per $100 of wages, the total premium paid by a city whose clerical staff earns $8,765,000 is MOST NEARLY

   A. $8,150   B. $81,515   C. $87,650   D. $93,765

27.____

28. Assume that a city council has approved a budget of $3,240,000,000 for the fiscal year beginning July 1, 2013. A city sales tax is expected to provide $1,100,000,000; licenses, fees, and sundry revenues are expected to yield $121,600,000; the balance is to be raised from property taxes. A tax equalization board has appraised all property in the city at a fair value of $42,500,000,000. The council wishes to assess property at 60% of its fair value.
The tax rate would need to be MOST NEARLY _____ per $100 of assessed value.

   A. $12.70   B. $10.65   C. $7.90   D. $4.00

28.____

29. The basic approach to a choice of alternatives is a method called

   A. linear programming
   B. incremental analysis
   C. total cost analysis
   D. general systems analysis

29.____

Questions 30-33.

DIRECTIONS: Answer Questions 30 through 33 on the basis of the following information.

Consider the following costs of a fire prevention program which can be funded at five different levels:

Funding Level	Annual Cost $(000)	Estimated Annual Property Loss $(000)	Lives Lost Per Year
A	0	2,000	5
B	100	1,000	3
C	500	500	1
D	1,000	250	3/4*
E	1,800	150	1/2

*I,e., three lives every four years.

30. If Choice C is made as against B, the payoff (excluding value of a life) is

   A. $0
   B. $100,000
   C. $300,000
   D. $500,000

30.____

31. If Choice D is made as against C, the IMPLICIT value of a human life is

   A. $250,000
   B. $750,000
   C. $1,000,000
   D. $1,333,333

31.____

32. The annual rate of return (exclusive of lives saved) on alternative C is MOST NEARLY

   A. 0%   B. 20%   C. 33%   D. 40%

32.____

33. Among the properties to be protected is a special high-risk group, such that 65% of the costs would be needed to avoid 25% of the loss.
    The return on that part of Alternative B applicable to this high-risk property class (exclusive of lives) would be MOST NEARLY

    A. 3.8   B. 16.25   C. 26   D. 90

    33.____

34. The following chart shows the number of persons employed in a certain industry for each year from 2007 through 2012.

	Thousands of employees
2007	5.7
2008	6.8
2009	7.0
2010	7.1
2011	7.4
2012	6.4

    In making a forecast of future trends, the one of the following steps which should be taken FIRST is to

    A. take the six-year average
    B. fit a curvilinear trend to the data
    C. fit a straight line, omitting 1982 as an *outlier,* i.e., as an unusually low reading
    D. check on what happened to the industry in 1982

    34.____

35. Of the following, the factor which is generally considered to be LEAST characteristic of a good control report is that it

    A. stresses performance that adheres to standard rather than emphasizing the exception
    B. supplies information intended to serve as the basis for corrective action
    C. provides feedback for the planning process
    D. includes data that reflect trends as well as current status

    35.____

36. Of the following concepts, the one which CANNOT be represented suitably by a pie chart is

    A. percent shares
    B. shares in absolute units
    C. time trends
    D. successive totals over time, with their shares

    36.____

37. A pictogram is ESSENTIALLY another version of a(n)_____ chart.

    A. plain bar   B. component bar
    C. pie   D. area

    37.____

38. A time series for a certain cost is presented in a graph. It is drawn so that the vertical (cost) axis starts at a point well above zero.
    This is a legitimate method of presentation for some purposes, but it may have the effect of

    38.____

A. hiding fixed components of the cost
B. exaggerating changes which, in actual amounts, may be insignificant
C. magnifying fixed components of the cost
D. impairing correlation analysis

39. Certain budgetary data may be represented by bar, area, or volume charts. Which one of the following BEST expresses the most appropriate order of usefulness?

A. Descends from bar to volume and area charts, the last two being about the same
B. Descends from volume to area to bar charts
C. Depends on the nature of the data presented
D. Descends from bar to area to volume charts

40. Among the original purposes of the governmental budgeting process, one hoped-for improvement which was LARGELY realized was

A. better managerial control over operations
B. legislative consideration of proposed expenditures in close correlation with revenue receipts
C. a budget balanced by a precise equivalence of taxes and expenditures
D. keeping government spending down

41. As used in systems analysis, the term *scenario* denotes a

A. policy
B. procedure
C. set of rules
D. primitive model

42. In budgeting, the quantification of tangible and intangible benefits

A. is legally required
B. has been done regularly since governmental budgeting was instituted
C. is difficult in most cases
D. requires only the setting of goals

43. When a time series is plotted on a ratio scale and comes out as an ascending straight line, it means that the dependent variable is increasing

A. by equal increments
B. at an increasing percentage rate
C. at a constant percentage rate
D. at a declining percentage rate

44. The one of the following ingredients of the scientific method which CANNOT be used in program analysis is that of

A. a complex hypothesis
B. a provable theory
C. computer simulation
D. repeated controlled experiments

45. When government budgeting was first introduced, it was attacked PRIMARILY as a(n)   45._____

    A. generator of excessive red tape
    B. power play by the legislative branch
    C. power play by the judicial branch
    D. example of creeping socialism

Questions 46-50.

DIRECTIONS: Answer Questions 46 through 50 on the basis of the information below.

Department XYZ
Size Distribution of Purchasing Orders

Amount of Order (dollars)	Number of Orders
1 - 9.99	91
10 - 19.99	135
20 - 49.99	320
50 - 99.99	712
100 - 199.99	1,050
200 - 499.99	735
500 - 999.99	305
1,000 - 1,999.99	94
2,000 - 4,999.99	36
5,000 - 9,999.99	18
10,000 - 19,999.99	3
20,000 - 49,000.99	1

46. The mode of this distribution of purchase orders is APPROXIMATELY   46._____

    A. $100   B. $150   C. $200   D. $1050

47. The median value is APPROXIMATELY   47._____

    A. $100   B. $150   C. $200   D. $1050

48. The value which falls at the tenth percentile is MOST NEARLY   48._____

    A. $21   B. $39   C. $45   D. $107

49. Suppose ten orders are added to each class interval below $1,000, but only one order is   49._____
    added in each interval $1,000 and above.
    Lacking more detailed information about them, we can estimate the total cost of these
    additional orders to be APPROXIMATELY

    A. $23,800   B. $76,100   C. $81,000   D. $123,800

50. Suppose that, in the original date, the first class interval given were specified as *less than $10* and the last two as *$10,000 and over.*
In that case, we would

    A. not be able to compute the mode
    B. not be able to compute the median
    C. not be able to compute the mean
    D. still be able to compute the mean, median, and mode

50.____

KEY (CORRECT ANSWERS)

1. C	11. A	21. C	31. C	41. D
2. B	12. D	22. D	32. B	42. C
3. B	13. A	23. A	33. B	43. C
4. D	14. D	24. A	34. D	44. D
5. B	15. A	25. B	35. A	45. A
6. D	16. C	26. B	36. C	46. B
7. B	17. C	27. B	37. A	47. B
8. A	18. C	28. C	38. B	48. B
9. D	19. A	29. B	39. D	49. B
10. C	20. B	30. B	40. A	50. C

EXAMINATION SECTION
TEST 1

DIRECTIONS: Each question or incomplete statement is followed by several suggested answers or completions. Select the one that BEST answers the question or completes the statement. *PRINT THE LETTER OF THE CORRECT ANSWER IN THE SPACE AT THE RIGHT.*

1. The task of developing data necessary for intelligent budgeting should be shared by the line department and the central budget agency.
   The central budget agency should provide data on

   A. manpower utilization   B. operating costs
   C. personnel needs   D. price and wage factors

   1.____

2. Under a system of responsibility accounting, the school transportation of handicapped children should be a charge against a department of

   A. child care   B. education
   C. health   D. transportation

   2.____

3. Cost-benefit analysis

   A. *can* always be expressed in dollars
   B. *can* seldom provide complete answers
   C. *should* always have a single criterion for evaluation
   D. *should* be restricted to factors that can be qualified

   3.____

4. Which measure among the following FAILS to relate programs to government objectives?

   A. Accident rates on highways
   B. Mortality rates
   C. Number of firemen per 1,000 population
   D. Unemployment rate

   4.____

5. The MOST difficult type of activity measurement is that of

   A. economy   B. effectiveness
   C. performance   D. production

   5.____

6. Assuming adequate authority and funds to support the decision, what would normally be the BEST method of coping with poor performance by units within a department?

   A. Appointing staff aides to the unit head, who can install better methods
   B. Assigning a team of administrative analysis from the central office to improve methods
   C. Replacing the unit head whenever a unit performs inadequately
   D. Training existing personnel in better management methods

   6.____

7. Of the following programs for methods improvement, the program that is likely to be MOST effective is

   A. employee suggestion awards
   B. production standards
   C. time study
   D. work simplification training

   7.____

8. In developing a program structure for PPBS, the one of the following that need NOT be a basic consideration is:

   A. All functions should be included regardless of organizational placement
   B. Classifications should focus on objectives
   C. Formal organization of government agencies need not correspond to program structure
   D. Program structures should be the same as budget categories

8.____

9. PERT is MOST closely related to

   A. Critical Path Method
   B. Efficiency and Economy Studies
   C. Operations Research
   D. Organization and Methods Studies

9.____

10. In PPBS, the role of the central budget bureau shifts from an emphasis on control to an emphasis on

    A. economy   B. efficiency
    C. management   D. policy

10.____

11. A properly administered budget should provide assurance that certain conditions will prevail.
    Which of the following is NOT appropriate to this statement?

    A. All agency heads will express their financial assumptions in the same terms.
    B. Diverse statements of expenses will be reviewed and coordinated by responsible officials.
    C. The agency head will be able to look to the budget director, after final acceptance of the budget, to defend and support his individual role and contribution to the overall budget plan.
    D. It will be possible to review and analyze variances between anticipated and actual financial results to determine what (if anything) went wrong.

11.____

12. The quality of a public service is MOST difficult to measure in terms of its

    A. characteristics   B. content
    C. payroll   D. objectives

12.____

13. In the analysis of processes, we are concerned with three types of variables: input, process, and output.
    Which of the following is a process variable?

    A. Social adaptation
    B. Student-teacher ratio
    C. Student time in classroom
    D. Teaching personnel

13.____

14. Which one of the following may BEST be considered an objective of BOTH the public and private sectors of the economy?

    A. Increasing the national income
    B. Maintaining a smoothly running free enterprise system by preserving competition
    C. Provision of public goods
    D. Redistribution of income

14.____

15. Which of the following methods of dealing with incorrect decisions on the part of subordinates is MOST constructive for the erring employee?

    A. Correct mistakes when they are found and say nothing
    B. Correct mistakes and warn the subordinate to be more careful
    C. Help the subordinate discern the nature of his errors
    D. Order the supervisor to review all decisions of his subordinates

16. In dealing with subordinates, some supervisors tend to issue orders which cannot be questioned or discussed.
    This method of supervision is likely to

    A. encourage open discussion and new ideas
    B. insure that subordinates clearly understand directions
    C. make the supervisor occasionally question his own decisions
    D. result in considerably faster action in completing an assignment

Questions 17-23.

DIRECTIONS: Questions 17 through 23 are to be answered SOLELY on the basis of the information contained in the following paragraphs, which is the fee schedule of a hypothetical college.

FEE SCHEDULE

a. A candidate for any baccalaureate degree is not required to pay tuition fees for undergraduate courses until he exceeds 128 credits. Candidates exceeding 128 credits in undergraduate courses are charged at the rate of $100 a credit for each credit of undergraduate course work in excess of 128. Candidates for a baccalaureate degree who are taking graduate courses must pay the same fee as any other student taking graduate courses.

b. Non-degree students and college graduates are charged tuition fees for courses, whether undergraduate or graduate, at the rate of $180 a credit. For such students there is an additional charge of $150 for each class hour per week in excess of the number of course credits. For example, if a three-credit course meets five hours a week, there is an additional charge for the extra two hours. Graduate courses are shown with a (G) before the course number.

c. All students are required to pay the laboratory fees indicated after the number of credits given for that course.

d. All students must pay a $250 general fee each semester.

e. Candidates for a baccalaureate degree are charged a $150 medical insurance fee for each semester. All other students are charged a $100 medical insurance fee each semester.

17. Miss Burton is not a candidate for a degree. She registers for the following courses in the spring semester: Economics 12, 4 hours a week, 3 credits; History (G) 23, 4 hours a week, 3 credits; English 1, 2 hours a week, 2 credits.
The TOTAL amount in fees that Miss Burton must pay is

   A. less than $2000
   B. at least $2000 but less than $2100
   C. at least $2100 but less than $2200
   D. $2200 or over

17.____

18. Miss Gray is not a candidate for a degree. She registers for the following courses in the fall semester: History 3, 3 hours a week, 3 credits; English 5, 3 hours a week, 2 credits; Physics 5, 6 hours a week, 3 credits, laboratory fee $60; Mathematics 7, 4 hours a week, 3 credits.
The TOTAL amount in fees that Miss Gray must pay is

   A. less than $3150
   B. at least $3150 but less than $3250
   C. at least $3250 but less than $3350
   D. $3350 or over

18.____

19. Mr. Wall is a candidate for the Bachelor of Arts degree and has completed 126 credits. He registers for the following courses in the spring semester, his final semester at college: French 4, 3 hours a week, 3 credits; Physics (G) 15, 6 hours a week, 3 credits, laboratory fee $80; History (G) 33, 4 hours a week, 3 credits.
The TOTAL amount in fees that this candidate must pay is

   A. less than $2100
   B. at least $2100 but less than $2300
   C. at least $2300 but less than $2500
   D. $2500 or over

19.____

20. Mr. Tindall, a candidate for the B.A. degree, has completed 122 credits of undergraduate courses. He registers for the following courses in his final semester: English 31, 3 hours a week, 3 credits; Philosophy 12, 4 hours a week, 4 credits; Anthropology 15, 3 hours a week, 3 credits; Economics (G) 68, 3 hours a week, 3 credits.
The TOTAL amount in fees that Mr. Tindall must pay in his final semester is

   A. less than $1200
   B. at least $1200 but less than $1400
   C. at least $1400 but less than $1600
   D. $1600 or over

20.____

21. Mr. Cantrell, who was graduated from the college a year ago, registers for graduate courses in the fall semester. Each course for which he registers carries the same number of credits as the number of hours a week it meets. If he pays a total of $1530 including a $100 laboratory fee, the number of credits for which he is registered is

   A. 4   B. 5   C. 6   D. 7

21.____

22. Miss Jayson, who is not a candidate for a degree, has registered for several courses including a lecture course in History. She withdraws from the course in History for which she had paid the required course fee of $690.
The number of hours that this course is scheduled to meet is

    A. 4   B. 5   C. 2   D. 3

22.____

23. Mr. Van Arsdale, a graduate of a college in Iowa, registers for the following courses in one semester: Chemistry 35, 5 hours a week, 3 credits; Biology 13, 4 hours a week, 3 credits, laboratory fee $150; Mathematics (G) 179, 3 hours a week, 3 credits.
The TOTAL amount in fees that Mr. Van Arsdale must pay is

    A. less than $2400
    B. at least $2400 but less than $2500
    C. at least $2500 but less than $2600
    D. at least $2600

23.____

24. Which of the following is LEAST important in successfully implementing organizational changes?

    A. Assigning responsibility for current failure
    B. Careful assessment of the *human consequences* of change
    C. Realistic goals for change
    D. Support and interest on the part of top management

24.____

25. Of the following, the one which is the MOST appropriate purpose for a conference of administrative staff in a government organization is to

    A. solve unusual and complex problems arising out of administrative reorganization in the agency
    B. provide detailed and specific information needed in the preparation of a study of proposed changes in departmental procedures
    C. check on progress in implementing recent changes in operating procedures in various divisions of the agency
    D. assign specific tasks to various individuals in connection with implementation of a new program

25.____

26. The MOST likely result of over-standardized and over-proceduralized regulations in an organization is

    A. deterioration of organizational structure
    B. inhibition of individual initiative
    C. resistance to delegation of authority
    D. resistance to the flow of communications

26.____

27. The concept that decision should be made at the lowest level in an organization where all the required information and competence are available is a GENERAL rule in

    A. communications theory
    B. decentralization of authority
    C. incremental decision-making
    D. span of control

27.____

28. The FIRST step in selecting a sample for a research project is to determine

    A. the characteristics of the population
    B. the extent to which you wish to generalize your findings
    C. the accessibility of the sample data
    D. whether every element of the population will have the same opportunity of being included in the sample

29. Direction, accompanied by authority, of the work of others is BEST defined as

    A. coordination
    B. domination
    C. planning
    D. supervision

30. Measures of central tendency, variability, and correlation of data are

    A. examples of descriptive statistics
    B. examples of inferential statistics
    C. procedures to determine the dependability of data
    D. unrelated statistics

31. In general, state and local debt in a state is incurred

    A. for the financing of capital acquisition and construction
    B. to balance all expense budget deficits
    C. when tax resistance is very high
    D. when tax resistance is relatively low

32. The MAJORITY of capital improvements undertaken by local governments are financed

    A. by borrowed funds
    B. by earmarked taxes
    C. by grants from higher levels of government
    D. on a pay-as-you-go basis

33. You have been asked to set up a system of reporting on activities to help the department's planning section. To propose as policy that no overlap or duplication be permitted, even if it meant that some areas of work would be left uncovered, would, GENERALLY, be

    A. *desirable;* overlapping and duplication in reporting indicates poor planning
    B. *undesirable;* inflexibility may result from establishment of general policy before the specific reporting system has been developed
    C. *desirable;* complete coverage is not essential in order to be able to plan operations
    D. *undesirable;* overlap or duplication is preferable to leaving a possible important area uncovered

34. PPBS CANNOT be applied if

    A. objectives are not comparable
    B. the difference in costs of two alternatives is very great
    C. there is a fixed budget ceiling
    D. utility is fixed

35. The BEST measure of effectiveness or results of a refuse collection program in terms of end products is the

   A. cleanliness of city streets
   B. number of men employed in the refuse collection process
   C. number of trucks used to collect refuse
   D. tons of refuse collected

36. Of the following, the budget process is MOST essentially concerned with

   A. allocating manpower to various units
   B. resolving the distribution of scarce resources among a variety of competing claims
   C. showing how much money is being spent for non-essentials
   D. showing which department is most efficient

37. The MAJOR value of performance budgeting is that it

   A. distinguishes between programs and performance
   B. enables program planning
   C. relates output to input
   D. requires the participation of top officials

38. The success of a budget allotment program depends PRIMARILY on the budget examiner's knowledge of

   A. departmental accounting procedures
   B. departmental budget codes
   C. seasonal patterns of departmental expenditures
   D. work flow charts of departmental activities

39. Costing of programs becomes MOST difficult when

   A. a program is conducted jointly by more than one agency
   B. performance cannot be measured in terms of end product
   C. salaries account for a major part of the program
   D. work standards do not exist

40. In analyzing the costs and benefits associated with a proposed municipal program, a budget examiner encounters certain factors which cannot be measured in dollar terms. His BEST course of action should be to

   A. assume that the non-measurable costs and benefits will balance out against one another
   B. give them weight equal to the weight given to measurable costs and benefits
   C. ignore such factors
   D. list them and describe what he believes their importance to be

KEY (CORRECT ANSWERS)

1. D	11. C	21. C	31. C
2. B	12. C	22. A	32. D
3. B	13. C	23. C	33. C
4. C	14. A	24. A	34. A
5. B	15. C	25. A	35. B
6. D	16. D	26. B	36. B
7. D	17. B	27. B	37. C
8. D	18. A	28. B	38. C
9. A	19. B	29. D	39. A
10. D	20. B	30. A	40. D

TEST 2

DIRECTIONS: Each question or incomplete statement is followed by several suggested answers or completions. Select the one that BEST answers the question or completes the statement. *PRINT THE LETTER OF THE CORRECT ANSWER IN THE SPACE AT THE RIGHT.*

1. A personnel utilization report for an activity indicates that efficiency for the fiscal year exceeded 100 percent. As a budget examiner, you may MOST logically infer that

    A. a study of the activity should be undertaken
    B. employees are overworked
    C. employees in this activity were very highly motivated
    D. the activity is well supervised

2. The one of the following which is LEAST likely to be a tool used by the budget examiner is

    A. analysis
    B. balance sheet
    C. economic forecast
    D. standards

3. In analyzing changes in productivity measured in terms of units per man-hour, it is NOT necessary to consider changes in

    A. price level
    B. quality of labor
    C. quality of output
    D. technology

4. In contrast with traditional object line-item budgeting, the PPBS information system MAINLY emphasizes

    A. measurement
    B. people
    C. projects
    D. purposes

5. It is estimated that prices will rise by 5 percent during the corning year. Interest on the current outstanding debt for the coming year may be expected to

    A. depend on new capital programs
    B. increase by about 5 percent
    C. increase by more than 5 percent because of the generally more rapid increase in construction costs
    D. remain unchanged

6. Which of the following terms BEST describes a tax that places a greater burden on those less able to pay than on those more able to pay? _____ tax.

    A. Escalator
    B. Progressive
    C. Regressive
    D. Reversal

7. The MOST important phase of the budget cycle, from a legal point of view, is

    A. appropriation
    B. classification
    C. execution
    D. formulation

8. The BEST reason for prescribing definite procedures for certain work in an agency is to   8._____

   A. enable supervision to keep on top of details of work
   B. enable work to be processed speedily and consistently
   C. prevent individual discretion
   D. reduce training periods

9. Good program planning should start with   9._____

   A. analysis of costs and benefits
   B. definition of objectives
   C. last year's program
   D. setting a top limit for spending

10. A decrease in manpower needs for an appropriation unit because of declining activity may BEST be provided for in the budget by   10._____

    A. a transfer of funds from other activities
    B. elimination of a vacant position
    C. elimination of backlog
    D. improved methods of work

11. Historical data are often used to estimate work standards.
    The MOST serious short-coming of this procedure is that it(s)   11._____

    A. involves the use of data difficult to obtain
    B. may tend to perpetuate existing inefficiencies
    C. requires an accurate accounting system
    D. use is difficult to sell to department officials

12. Of the following, the one which is NOT a basic concept of administrative organization is to   12._____

    A. assemble jobs into units which serve a common goal
    B. group like functions into the same job or jobs
    C. provide appropriate lines of authority and communication
    D. replace men with machines wherever machines can be built to do the work

13. Within organizations, the BASIC functions of communication are to   13._____

    A. build a permanent record of the organizational activities
    B. give and receive directions and information
    C. stimulate closer relationships between management and workers
    D. inform each employee of all significant events which may affect the organization

14. Automatic data processing does NOT necessarily   14._____

    A. assure more valid results
    B. facilitate data handling
    C. permit extensive manipulation of data
    D. permit the use of complex models of activities

15. The head of the agency has issued instructions that employees preparing letters for his signature use no more words than are needed to convey adequately the required information.
    To follow this rule in letter writing is GENERALLY

    A. *desirable;* typing of the correspondence will be less time-consuming
    B. *undesirable;* letters will be so terse that unfavorable attitudes toward government agencies may result
    C. *desirable;* the purpose of the letter will be carried out without obscuring the meaning or tiring the reader
    D. *undesirable;* it is usually necessary to elaborate on an explanation in order to make sure that the reader will understand the meaning

16. When preparing a long report on a study prepared for your superior, the one of the following which should usually come FIRST in your report is a(n)

    A. brief description of the working procedure followed in your study
    B. review of the background conditions leading to the study
    C. summary of your conclusions
    D. outline of suggested procedures for implementing the report

17. The MAIN function of a research report is usually to

    A. convince the reader of the adequacy of the research
    B. report as expeditiously as possible what was done, why it was done, the results, and the conclusions
    C. contribute to the body of scientific knowledge
    D. substantiate an a priori conclusion by presenting a set of persuasive quantitative data

18. Which one of the following terms BEST describes operating agencies which directly serve the public?

    A. Administrative   B. Line
    C. Specialist   D. Staff

19. The budget in a democracy is primarily an expression of which one of the following types of authority?

    A. Administrative   B. Executive
    C. Legislative   D. Managerial

20. The *item veto,* as applied to budgeting, is the

    A. power of the chief executive to veto legislative riders
    B. power of the chief executive to veto the entire appropriation bill
    C. requirement for a chief executive to itemize the reasons for his veto of the appropriation bill
    D. right of a chief executive to approve an appropriation bill as a whole but disapprove certain details

21. An experiment was conducted to measure the error rate of typists. The results follows: 21.____

TYPISTS	PERCENT OF TOTAL OUTPUT	ERROR RATE (IN PERCENT)
A	30	1.00
B	30	1.50
C	40	0.50

The error rate, in percent, for the three typists combined

   A. is 0.95
   B. is 1.00
   C. is 3.00
   D. cannot be calculated from the given data

22. It is found that for the past three years the average weekly number of inspections per inspector ranged from 20 inspections to 40 inspections. 22.____
    On the basis of this information, it is MOST reasonable to conclude that

   A. on the average, 30 inspections per week were made
   B. the average weekly number of inspections never fell below 20
   C. the performance of inspectors deteriorated over the three year period
   D. the range in average weekly inspections was 60

Questions 23-25.

DIRECTIONS: Questions 23 through 25 are to be answered on the basis of the following information.

The number of students admitted to University X in 2018 from High School Y was 268 students. This represented 13.7 percent of University X's entering freshman classes. In 2019, it is expected that University X will admit 591 students from High School Y, which is expected to represent 19.4 percent of the 2019 entering freshman classes of University X.

23. Which of the following is the CLOSEST estimate of the size of University X's expected 2019 entering freshman classes? 23.____
    _____ students.

   A. 2000   B. 2500   C. 3000   D. 3500

24. Of the following, the expected percentage of increase from 2018 to 2019 in the number of students graduating from High School Y and entering University X as freshmen is HOST NEARLY 24.____

   A. 5.7%   B. 20%   C. 45%   D. 120%

25. Assume that the cost of processing each freshman admission to University X from High School Y in 2018 was an average of $28. Also, that this was 1/3 more than the average cost of processing each of the other 2018 freshman admissions to University X. 25.____
    Then, the one of the following that MOST closely shows the total processing cost of all 2018 freshman admissions to University X is

   A. $6,500   B. $20,000   C. $30,000   D. $40,000

Questions 26-28.

DIRECTIONS: Answer Questions 26 through 28 on the basis of the following information.

Assume that in order to encourage Program A, the State and Federal governments have agreed to make the following reimbursements for money spent on Program A, provided the unreimbursed balance is paid from City funds.

During Fiscal Year 2018-2019 - For the first $2 million expended, 50% Federal reimbursement and 30% State reimbursement; for the next $3 million, 40% Federal reimbursement and 20% State reimbursement; for the next $5 million, 20% Federal reimbursement and 10% State reimbursement. Above $10 million expended, no Federal or State reimbursement.

During Fiscal Year 2019-2020 - For the first $1 million expended, 30% Federal reimbursement and 20% State reimbursement; for the next $4 million, 15% Federal reimbursement and 10% State reimbursement. Above $5 million expended, no Federal or State reimbursement.

26. Assume that the Program A expenditures are such that the State reimbursement for Fiscal Year 2018-2019 will be $1 million.
    Then, the Federal reimbursement for Fiscal Year 2018-2019 will be

    A. $1,600,000   B. $1,800,000
    C. $2,000,000   D. $2,600,000

27. Assume that $8 million were to be spent on Program A in Fiscal Year 2019-2020, the total amount of unreimbursed City funds required would be

    A. $3,500,000   B. $4,500,000
    C. $5,500,000   D. $6,500,000

28. Assume that the City desires to have a combined total of $6 million spent in Program A during both the Fiscal Year 2018-2019 and the Fiscal Year 2019-2020.
    Of the following expenditure combinations, the one which results in the GREATEST reimbursement of City funds is _____ million in Fiscal Year 2018-2019 and _____ million in Fiscal Year 2019-2020.

    A. $5; $1   B. $4; $2   C. $3; $3   D. $2; $4

29. The term *PPBS* relates most directly to one of the systems PRINCIPALLY designed to do which one of the following?

    A. Reduce the number of mistakes resulting in spoilage and wasted effort to zero
    B. Obtain greater cost effectiveness
    C. Assure that all operations are performed at the highest quality level that is technically attainable at the present time
    D. Assure that all output units are fully verified prior to being sent out

30. Assume that you are working with a computer programmer to solve a complex problem. Together, you have defined your problem in everyday English clearly enough to proceed. In the next step, you both start breaking down the information in the definition so that you both can decide on the operations needed for programming the problem.
    This next step of getting from the definition of the problem to the point where you can begin laying out the steps actually to be taken in solving the problem is MOST appropriately called

A. completing the documentation B. implementing the solution
C. identifying the problem statement D. analyzing the problem

31. Assume that during the fiscal year 2018-2019, a bureau produced 20% more work units than it produced in the fiscal year 2017-2018. Also, assume that during the fiscal year 2018-2019 that bureau's staff was 20% SMALLER than it was in the fiscal year 2017-2018.
On the basis of this information, it would be MOST proper to conclude that the number of work units produced per staff member in that bureau in the fiscal year 2018-2019 exceeded the number of work units produced per staff member in that bureau in the fiscal year 2017-2018 by which one of the following percentages?

A. 20% B. 25% C. 40% D. 50%

31.____

32. Assume that during the following five fiscal years (FY), a bureau has received the following appropriations:
    FY 2014-2015 - $200,000
    FY 2015-2016 - $240,000
    FY 2016-2017 - $280,000
    FY 2017-2018 - $390,000
    FY 2018-2019 - $505,000
The bureau's appropriation for which one of the following fiscal years showed the LARGEST percentage of increase over the bureau's appropriation for the immediately previous fiscal year?
FY

A. 2015-2016 B. 2016-2017 C. 2017-2018 D. 2018-2019

32.____

33. Which one of the following statements is MOST generally supported by modern industrial and behavioral research?

A. High productivity and high quality each show a substantial negative correlation with high morale.
B. Where professional employees participate in defining how much and what caliber of their service should be considered acceptable, they generally will set both types of goals substantially below those which management alone would have set.
C. Professional employees get greatest satisfaction out of work that challenges them to exert their capacities fully.
D. The participative approach to management relieves the manager of the need to be a decision-maker.

33.____

34. A bureau has a very large number of clerical personnel engaged in very similar duties, and only a limited portion can be absent at any one time if the workload is to be handled properly.
Which one of the following would generally be the bureau head's BEST approach toward scheduling the annual leave time (vacation, etc.) to be taken by the employees of that bureau?
The bureau head

A. personally receives from each employee his preferred schedule of leave time, personally decides on when the employee can most conveniently be spared from the viewpoint of the office workload, and issues his decisions to all concerned in the form of a binding memorandum

34.____

B. advises his subordinate supervisors and employees of the parameters and constraints in time and numbers upon annual leave. The employees and subordinate supervisors prepare a proposed annual leave schedule within those limitations and submit it to the bureau head for approval or modification, and for promulgation
C. initially asks his subordinate supervisors to prepare a proposed annual leave schedule for employees with a minimum of consultation with the employees. He then circulates this schedule to the employees over his signature as a proposed schedule and invites employee reaction directly to him
D. asks employee or union representatives to prepare a proposed schedule with all leave to be taken spread evenly over the entire vacation period. He personally reviews and accepts or modifies this proposal,

35. An agency head desires to have an estimate of the *potential* of a middle-level administrative employee for development for higher-level administrative positions. He also desires to try to minimize possible errors or capriciousness which might creep into that estimate. Of the following, it would generally be MOST desirable to have the estimate

   A. result from the pooled judgment of three or more past or present substantial-level supervisors of the subject employee and of persons with lateral or service contacts with the subject employee
   B. made solely by substantial-level executives outside the past or present direct line of supervision above the subject employee
   C. result from the pooled judgment of substantial-level personnel staff members rather than line executives
   D. made solely by the present immediate line supervisor of the subject employee

36. If we total all of the occasions in which all government positions are filled with new faces (persons who did not occupy those specific positions previously), we generally would find that a GREATER number will result from

   A. new accessions from the outside than from movement of personnel within the organization
   B. movement of personnel within the organization than from new accessions from the outside
   C. promotion of staff personnel to higher staff jobs than from promotion of line personnel to higher line jobs
   D. filling of Exempt and Non-Competitive Class positions than from filling of Competitive Class positions

37. Which one of the following is generally the BEST criterion for determining the classification title to which a position should be allocated?
    The

   A. personal qualifications possessed by the present or expected appointee to the position
   B. consequences of the work of the position or the responsibility it carries
   C. number of work units required to be produced or completed in the position
   D. consequences of inadequate overall governmental pay scales upon recruitment of outstanding personnel

38. The MAJOR decisions as to which jobs shall be created and who shall carry which responsibilities should generally be made by

    A. budgetary advisers
    B. line managers
    C. classification specialists
    D. peer-level rating committee

39. Which one of the following generally BEST characterizes the basic nature of budget making and budget administration from a managerial viewpoint?

    A. Budget administration is control, while budget making is planning.
    B. Budget administration is planning, while budget making is control.
    C. Both budget making and budget administration are only control functions; neither is a planning function.
    D. Both budget making and budget administration are only planning functions; neither is a control function.

40. In preparing his annual budget request for a large bureau with both substantial continuing and anticipated new activities, the bureau head must consider various factors (e.g., retaining credibility and obtaining required funds).
    Of the following, the BEST long-range budgeting strategy would normally be for the bureau head to request

    A. twice what is actually needed on the assumption that higher authorities will generally cut the requested amount in half
    B. ten percent less than he actually estimates to be needed and to submit a supplementary request later for that ten percent
    C. what is needed for the continuing activities plus twenty-five percent to allow some slack funds
    D. what he estimates is needed to continue existing essential programs and to fund needed new activities

KEY (CORRECT ANSWERS)

1. A	11. B	21. A	31. D
2. B	12. D	22. B	32. C
3. A	13. B	23. C	33. C
4. D	14. A	24. D	34. B
5. D	15. C	25. D	35. A
6. C	16. C	26. B	36. B
7. A	17. B	27. D	37. B
8. B	18. B	28. A	38. B
9. B	19. C	29. B	39. A
10. B	20. D	30. D	40. D

EXAMINATION SECTION
TEST 1

DIRECTIONS: Each question or incomplete statement is followed by several suggested answers or completions. Select the one that *BEST* answers the question or completes the statement. *PRINT THE LETTER OF THE CORRECT ANSWER IN THE SPACE AT THE RIGHT.*

1. An analyst is writing a report dealing with the distribution of deaths caused by various types of cardiovascular diseases. He decides to facilitate the reader's grasp of the information presented by including in the report a device that permits comparison of parts to each other, and to the whole at the same time.
   Of the following, the *MOST* appropriate and efficient device he should use for this purpose is the

   A. graph
   B. pie diagram
   C. flow sheet
   D. line chart with one series

   1.____

2. In carrying out a cost-effectiveness analysis, the analyst should follow certain guidelines. The *MOST* important of these guidelines involves the

   A. utilization of both the fixed utility approach and the fixed budget approach
   B. proper structuring of the problem and design of the analysis
   C. necessity of building a model that is highly formal and mathematical
   D. provision for implicit treatment of uncertainty

   2.____

3. In a decision which involves fairness -- such as assigning new office equipment to workers when the agency does not receive enough new office equipment for the entire group -- the *PRIMARY* determinant of the decision's effectiveness will be the

   A. systematic or traditional approach which is emphasized in reaching the decision
   B. random nature of the assignment
   C. feedback a decisionmaker receives concerning the decision
   D. acceptance of the decision by the persons who have to execute it

   3.____

4. In order to give line personnel some insight into staff problems and vice versa it has been suggested that line and staff assignments within a particular city agency be rotated. Which of the following criticisms would be *MOST* valid for opposing such a proposal?

   A. Generally speaking, line and staff personnel have different perspectives on organizational structures which makes rotation in assignments extremely difficult.
   B. Since their educational backgrounds are often quite diverse, staff personnel are often at a disadvantage when serving in line assignments.
   C. Line personnel frequently resent having to perform the more difficult tasks that staff assignments entail.
   D. Serving in a rotating assignment may not necessarily provide the personnel with any significant degree of insight as anticipated.

   4.____

5. Which one of the following approaches to criticism of a subordinate or associate is *generally* the *MOST* appropriate and effective?
   Criticize

   A. by making a comparison with a more exemplary employee

   5.____

53

B. the act, not the person
C. in a humorous vein
D. in general rather than specific terms

6. Assume that two policy units have been formed to study the impact of Federal programs in the city. The two units operate in an essentially similar manner, except for their communications procedures. In unit A any member may communicate and exchange information with any other member of the unit; in unit B a member may only communicate information with the unit supervisor.
In evaluating the effect that these communications procedures have on the level of productivity, it will *generally* be found that

   A. unit A's level of productivity will be greater than unit B's level of productivity for simple problems
   B. unit B's level of productivity will be greater than unit A's level of productivity for simple problems
   C. initial levels of profuctivity are higher in unit A than unit B for complex problems
   D. initial levels of productivity are higher in unit B than in unit A for complex problems

7. In the process of communicating an idea, the following five distinct steps are generally involved:
   I. Selection of a media and transmission of the message
   II. Decoding of a message, i.e., meaning is extracted from the message
   III. Message is received
   IV. Idea is organized into a series of symbols designed to give meaning
   V. Action is taken and/or feedback is given

   In what logical, sequential order should these steps be arranged for effective two-way communications to take place?

   A. V, I, II, III, IV   B. II, I, III, IV, V
   C. IV, I, III, II, V   D. I, III, IV, II, V

8. Informal employee groups that share certain norms and strive for member satisfaction through the achievement of group goals are known as work groups.
Which of the following statements can *generally* be considered as being *FALSE* in describing work groups in a moderate size organization?

   A. Formation of work groups is ubiquitous and inevitable.
   B. Work groups strongly influence the overall behavior and performance of their members.
   C. An organization can reap positive and negative consequences as a result of work groups.
   D. Elimination of work groups can be easily achieved by management pressure.

9. Under the management approach known as *management by objectives* which of the following criteria is *generally* used to determine whether the manager has been successful?

   A. Activities performed
   B. Results achieved
   C. Production schedules completed
   D. Financial savings accomplished

10. Of the following, the MOST accurate statement relative to job attitudes is that they

    A. cannot be influenced by only one person
    B. are always the result of work groups
    C. have no relationship to productivity
    D. are strongly influenced by work situation

11. Assume that measures to overcome a budget deficit, including attrition and a hiring freeze, have significantly decreased the work-output of a city agency. The agency administrator desires to develop a plan to restore production to its former level by increasing the work-load and responsibility of the agency's employees.
    In order to obtain *maximum* employee cooperation and *minimize* employee resistance, it would be MOST advisable for the

    A. administrator of the agency to personally describe to the employees the new work changes that they are to follow
    B. employees to decide what the optimal changes in the work load should be
    C. management representatives to consult with employee representatives on these matters
    D. immediate supervisor of the employees to decide on the work changes to be implemented

12. Eliciting the support and cooperation of others often requires a great deal of persuasion. Which one of the following persuasive techniques or practices is generally the LEAST desirable for you, an analyst, to use?

    A. Establish your expertness and authority
    B. Present your arguments without emotion
    C. In presenting your arguments, express yourself in the manner to which you are accustomed
    D. Try to find a face-saving way for your opponent to change his/her mind

13. The following illustration depicts the structure of a municipal agency.

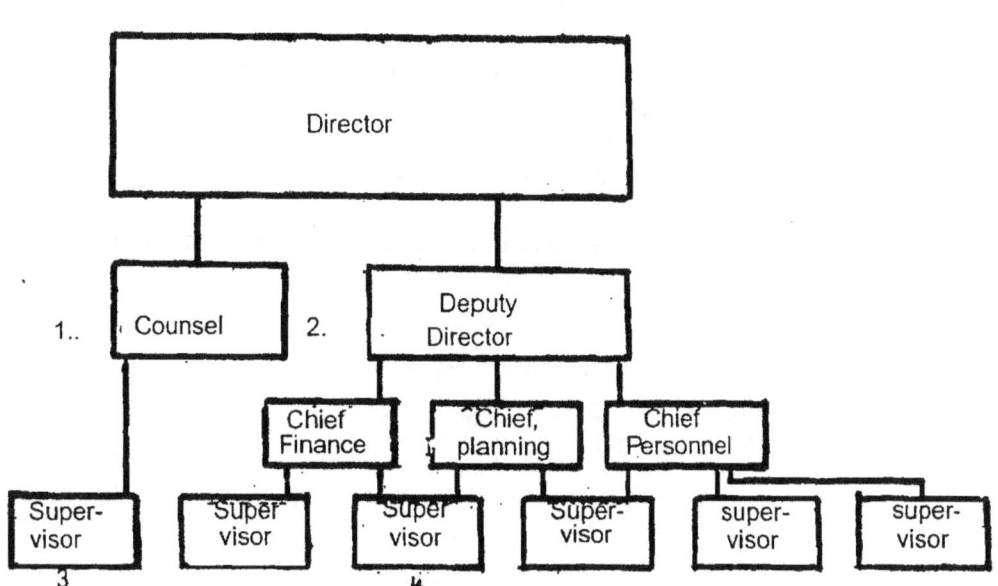

In the above illustration, which individual would generally be expected to encounter the MOST difficulty in carrying out his organizational functions?

    A. 1   B. 2   C. 3   D. 4

14. An agency in which a free flow of communication exists is an agency in which no barriers or structures are erected to control or bar the flow of information and messages between and among management and staff, horizontally or vertically.
    Of the following, the GREATEST disadvantage that would be most likely to occur in an agency in which such a free flow of communication exists, is that

    A. it would be difficult to determine which information is important and which is irrelevant
    B. there would be a lesser degree of staff-employee participation and cooperation in communicating
    C. more restrictive controls would be placed on managerial employees
    D. important communications would tend to be eliminated, and and trivial communications over-emphasized

15. Feedback is generally considered an essential factor in oral communication MAINLY because

    A. it enables the speaker to know whether he is understood
    B. the speed of communication is accelerated
    C. it eliminates the necessity of the speaker to use gestures and facial expressions when speaking
    D. the listener is unable to immediately respond to the speaker until the latter is finished

16. Assume that two employees are working on a joint project and they have a difference of opinion on the methodology to be used. Each employee not only listens to the other's opinion on methodology but projects him-self into the other's position.
    This type of listening is *usually* considered

    A. *ineffective,* mainly because it will be impossible for the employees to reach a satisfactory agreement
    B. *effective,* mainly because each employee will then be more critical of the other's argument
    C. *ineffective,* mainly because each worker will unconsciously and unintentionally accept the other's viewpoint
    D. *effective,* mainly because each speaker can understand the other's viewpoint and can then respond intelligently to his remarks

17. The arithmetic mean is commonly used in describing data. Which one of the following statements is NOT true about the arithmetic mean?

    A. It is a measure of dispersion.
    B. The sum of the deviations around it is zero.
    C. It is easy to compute, understand and recognize.
    D. It may be treated alegebraically.

Questions 18 - 20.

DIRECTIONS: Answer Questions 18 through 20 on the basis of the following data. Assume that you are using these data in assessing the impact of Federal and State income taxes on New York City residents, and comparing it to the effect of Federal and State taxes in other areas.

EFFECT OF DEDUCTIBILITY (i.e., deductibility of taxes levied by other jurisdictions in calculating the net base of the tax in the taxing jurisdiction.)

Net income before personal exemption	Effective rate of tax				
	Federal (assuming no state tax)	State		Combined Federal and State	
		New York*	Minnesota (assuming no federal tax)	New York	Minnesota
	(1)	(2)	(3)	(4)	(5)
$20,000	25.0	4.1	6.9	27.6	27.9
50,000	42.2	5.4	9.1	44.0	43.9
100,000	56.0	5.9	9.8	57.5	57.1
200,000	69.2	6.1	10.1	69.9	69.5
1,500,000	88.0	6.3	10.5	89.3	88.9

*New York has no deductibility; the Federal government has deductibility.

18. In which of the following columns is the tax rate shown to be the *LEAST* progressive?   18.____

   A. 1   B. 2   C. 4   D. 5

19. Which of the following statements is *TRUE* about the reasons why Columns 1 and 2 do not equal Column 4 for each salary level?   19.____

   A. Personal deductions are taken into account in Column 4 but not in Columns 1 and 2.
   B. Federal deducibility of state taxes only is taken into account in Column 4 but not in Columns 1 and 2.
   C. Reciprocal deductibility is taken into account in Column 4 but not in Columns 1 and 2.
   D. State deductibility of federal taxes only is taken into account in Column 4 but not in Columns 1 and 2.

20. The *EFFECT* of the State's introducing deductibility, given that the Federal government maintains deductibility, is to   20.____

   A. *increase* Federal and State income
   B. *decrease* Federal and State income
   C. *decrease* Federal income and increase State income
   D. *increase* Federal income and decrease State income

21. Assume that you have been made project coordinator for a study concerning the implementation of casino gambling in the city. You have assigned each of the professional staff members simple tasks in specialized areas for the duration of the project. For you to make such job assignments would *generally* be

    A. *desirable;* the performance of simple tasks will motivate individuals to work diligently
    B. *desirable;* specialized tasks induce a sense of accomplishment to individuals
    C. *undesirable;* specialized tasks are more difficult to learn
    D. *undesirable;* specialized tasks may lead to a loss of feeling of accomplishment

22. Assume that you have been asked to submit a proposal for the reorganization of a unit that is charged with performing difficult nonroutine work. Frequently decisions must be made quickly and concurrence obtained from high-level agency heads.
    Given the above conditions, of the following it would be MOST logical to structure the organization

    A. on the basis of a relatively wide span of control
    B. on the basis of a relatively narrow span of control
    C. with many organizational levels with a wide span of control
    D. with more emphasis on line than staff units

23. Assume that a study has indicated that a recently created city *superagency* has had formal communication difficulties among various component agencies. It appears that jurisdictional overlapping among those agencies has caused frequent rerouting and unnecessary duplication of communications within the organization. Which one of the following proposals would MOST effectively deal with the communications problem encountered by this *superagency*?

    A. Create a central communications office to handle all communications for this *superagency.*
    B. Duplicate and distribute all communications to each component within this *superagency.*
    C. Reduce the overlapping areas of jurisdiction among the component agencies
    D. Decentralize the *superagency* on a *borough* basis to expedite mail delivery

24. The utilization of input-output concepts in connection with the application of the systems concept to government raises the problem of the quantification of objectives and performance (the value of the public benefit). The one of the following which is MOST easily *quantifiable* is

    A. education
    B. police service
    C. subway car maintenance
    D. the effectiveness of a welfare administrator

25. When an analyst tries to conceive of a city management problem as a *systems* problem, he is, first of all, confronted with establishing the boundaries of the system. Of the following, the city problem which can *most likely* be conceived of within a system whose boundaries are roughly equivalent to those of the city is

    A. taxation
    B. welfare
    C. fire protection
    D. transportation

25.____

KEY (CORRECT ANSWERS)

1.	B		11.	C
2.	B		12.	B
3.	D		13.	D
4.	D		14.	A
5.	B		15.	A
6.	C		16.	D
7.	C		17.	A
8.	D		18.	B
9.	B		19.	B
10.	D		20.	D

21.	D
22.	B
23.	C
24.	C
25.	C

TEST 2

DIRECTIONS: Each question or incomplete statement is followed by several suggested answers or completions. Select the one that *BEST* answers the question or completes the statement. *PRINT THE LETTER OF THE CORRECT ANSWER IN THE SPACE AT THE RIGHT.*

1. When installing a new *system,* an analyst may choose among several types of installation plans - the *all-at-once type,* the *piecemeal type,* or the *parallel type* each suited to a particular problem or degree of complexity in the system.
   The one of the following situations in which the *parallel type* would be *MOST* appropriate is a situation

   A. in which a minimum installation cost is required
   B. involving a small volume of transactions
   C. in which the change is not radical or does not involve new machines
   D. involving large installation projects and intricate processing

2. Many decision situations involve a great deal of uncertainty about the future, which is difficult to take into account in the analysis of alternatives. One technique developed for treating such uncertainty is designed to measure the possible effects on alternatives under analysis resulting from variations in uncertain elements. The analyst uses several *expected values* for uncertain parameters in an attempt to ascertain how the results vary (i.e., the relative ranking of the alternatives under consideration) in light of variations in the uncertain parameters. The analyst attempts to determine the alternative (or feasible combination of alternatives) likely to achieve a specified objective, gain or utility at the lowest cost. The one of the following which *BEST* describes the above technique is:

   A. Contingency analysis employing the fixed-budget approach
   B. Contingency analysis employing the fixed-benefits approach
   C. Sensitivity analysis employing the fixed-budget approach
   D. Sensitivity analysis employing the fixed-benefits approach

3. In general, the analytical techniques of management science are of the *LEAST* value when

   A. the effects of a small number of controlled variables must be considered
   B. the number of relevant uncontrolled variables is small
   C. relevant causes and effects are factual in nature and can be stated and measured numerically or symbolically
   D. There are reasons to believe that past relationships will continue to hold in the future

4. During the installation period of a new system, tight controls must be maintained over every phase of the operation. To do this, an analyst may set up a *warning system* within the system which forecasts potential bottle-necks and affords sufficient clues for correcting any problems, errors or fall-downs.
   The one of the following control devices or techniques which would be *most likely* to involve extra effort during the installation, and slow down the processing time is

A. paper flow controls - log sheets, numerical controls, etc. (a system of logging input and output)
B. timing controls - to inform the analyst about the proper time interval between certain activities with-in the systems
C. program check points - a periodic review of processing to date at each check point
D. accounting control totals, to accumulate invoice numbers as the first and last steps in the system and compare the totals

5. Which of the following types of work measurement techniques would be *MOST* appropriate for obtaining details of a particular job for cost analysis purposes, such as the operating costs of various types of duplicating machines?

    A. Work sampling
    B. Predetermined time standards
    C. The time study (stop-watch timing)
    D. Historical

6. It is anticipated that a certain cancer detection program will be capable of detecting many cases at an early stage and that society will be thus enabled to cure twice as many cases as it cures currently. The benefits to society include the reduction in cost of hospitalization, etc., that would have been incurred otherwise.
Benefits such as a reduction in the cost of hospitalization are *most usually* called

    A. direct benefits
    B. secondary benefits
    C. intergenerational benefits
    D. external benefits

7. The results of departmental and agency programs can be measured in terms of *EFFECTIVENESS* or *BENEFITS*. Thus, careful budget preparation will permit the calculation of costs which can then be compared, or equated, to these results. Which one of the following statements pertaining to cost-effectiveness measurements is *MOST* valid?

    A. In cost-effectiveness measurements, a dollar value is assigned to the output.
    B. The measurement is expressed in terms of quality of output for a given cost.
    C. Cost effectiveness ratios express the relationship between the costs of programs
    D. A cost-effectiveness measurement will show the number of outputs which can be achieved for the expenditure of a given amount of money.

8. Assume that you have been asked to evaluate personnel programs in four city agencies The statistical test that would be *MOST* appropriate for testing the significance of the differences in the mean number of days absent (normality may be assumed) during the year 2004 in four different agencies is the

    A. one-way analysis of variance
    B. standard deviation
    C. regression analysis
    D. Chi-square test (x^2-test)

9. Assume that you have been asked to evaluate differences in the children just enrolled in two youth programs. In reviewing the relevant published material you find that in one particular study involving two groups, N = 9 and N = 13, there is a significant difference in the mean scores of the two groups on a characteristic which you believe to be normally distributed.
   The statistical test *most likely* used in this study to determine the significance of the difference in the means of the two groups on this characteristic is the

   A. Chi-square test (x2-test)
   B. Pearson Product-Moment correlation (r)
   C. t-test
   D. two-way analysis of variance

10. In statistics, three common measures of central tendency are the mean, median and mode.
    For which of the following conditions would the median generally be the *BEST* choice to use? When the

    A. distribution of scores is skewed
    B. scores are distributed symmetrically around a central point
    C. standard deviation must also be calculated
    D. most frequently occurring value is required

11. Nonparametric statistical tests are *usually* employed when

    A. large samples are used
    B. a very powerful or exact test is needed
    C. data cannot be expressed in ranks
    D. a normally distributed population cannot be assumed

12. Assume that in a report presented to you by an employee under your supervision, a coefficient of correlation of +1.73 is reported between the age at which one first smokes cigarettes and the age at which one first smokes marijuana.
    You should *most reasonably* interpret this figure to mean there is a

    A. strong positive correlation
    B. weak positive correlation
    C. weak negative correlation
    D. typographical error

13. One of the major research techniques most often used in studies of organizational behavior problems is the survey. An analyst who utilizes the survey technique should be aware that its *MAJOR* drawback is

    A. the lack of depth obtained from the two major data-collection tolls used in surveys: the mailed question-naire and the personal interview
    B. its impracticality in assessing or estimating the present state of affairs with regard to a variable that changes over time for a large group of subjects
    C. the restriction of this technique to a single, or very few, units of analysis
    D. its absence of dependence upon the collection of empirical data

14. In order for an analyst to understand and interpret statistical data he/she must understand which types of data tend to approximate the normal probability curve, i.e., are normally distributed.
Which of the following types of data falls into this category?
Frequency of

   A. educational test scores for students of a given age, plotted against test score
   B. filing of income tax returns for citizens of a given age, plotted against date of filing
   C. deaths due to childhood disease plotted against age
   D. deaths due to degenerative diseases, plotted against age

14.____

15. Which of the following terms describes a line or curve formed by plotting employees salaries that increase yearly by a fixed percentage over the previous year? (In answering the question, assume that time is on the horizontal axis (abscissa) and salary is on the vertical axis (ordinate) - both axes are marked linearly.)

   A. Linear (increasing at a constant rate)
   B. Positively accelerating (increasing at an increasing rate)
   C. Negatively accelerating (increasing at a decreasing rate)
   D. Negatively decelerating (decreasing at a decreasing rate)

15.____

Questions 16 - 17

DIRECTIONS: Answer Questions 16 and 17 on the basis of the following groups, both of which depict the same information in different ways.

The x and y axes in graphs A and B are not necessarily drawn in the same scale. The points along the curves on both graphs represent corresponding points, and are the upper limits of class intervals.

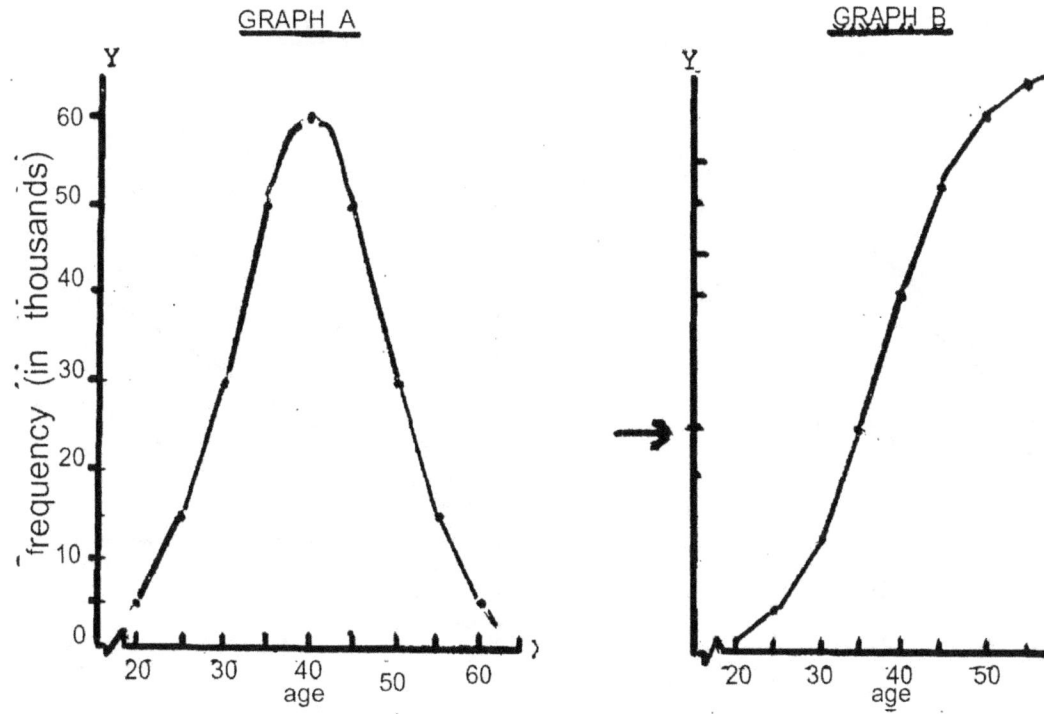

16. The ordinate (y-axis) in graph B is

    A. frequency
    B. cumulative frequency
    C. average frequency
    D. log frequency

17. The arrow on the y-axis in graph B indicates a particular number. That number is, *most nearly*

    A. 100   B. 50,000   C. 100,000   D. 150,000

Questions 18 - 19

DIRECTIONS: Answer Questions 18 and 19 on the basis of the graphs that appear on the following page.

18. In Graph I, the vertical distance between lines E and T within the crosshatched area represents the

    A. savings to the city if work of less than 50 miles is performed by the city
    B. loss to the city if work of less than 50 miles is performed by the city
    C. savings to the city if work of more than 50 miles is performed by the city
    D. loss to the city if work of more than 50 miles is performed by the city

19. Graph II is identical to Graph I except that contractor costs have been eliminated. Total costs (line E) are the sum of fixed costs (line F) and variable costs. Variable costs are represented by line

    A. A   B. B   C. C   D. D

ROAD REPAIR COSTS IF PERFORMED BY CITY STAFF OR AN OUTSIDE CONTRACTOR

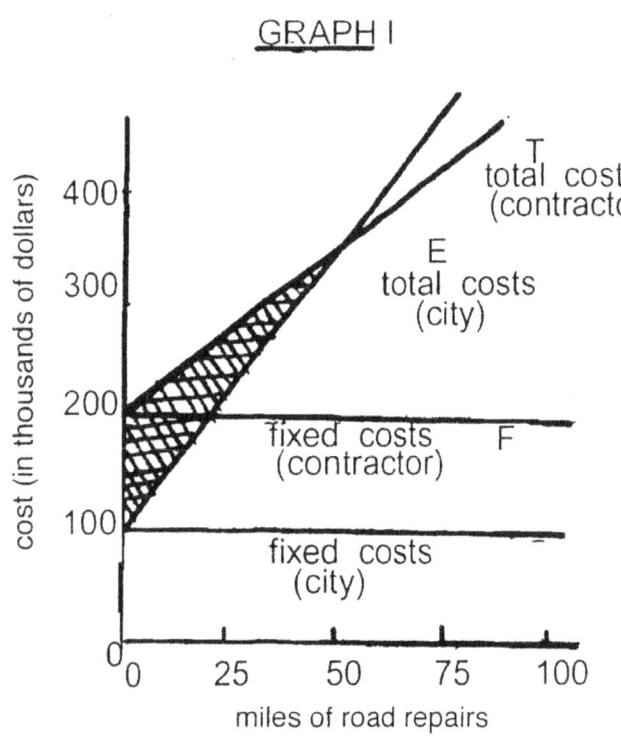

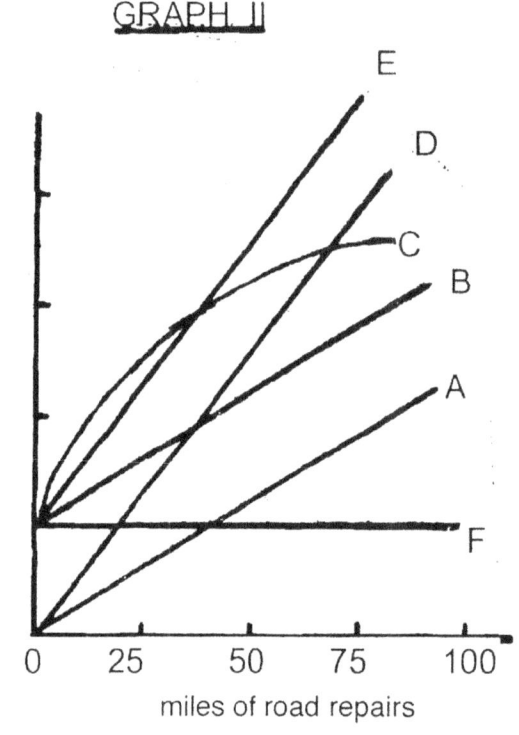

20. Fiscal experts in municipal affairs have contended that the most acute problem facing the city today seems to be the growth of the city's short-term debt.
Of the following, the LEAST likely reason for the city to engage in short-term borrowing is that the city

    A. expects money from long-term borrowing that it plans to undertake
    B. needs to be tided over until funds due from the Federal or State government arrive
    C. needs money to finance big construction outlays
    D. anticipates money from future tax collections

21. A MAJOR criticism of the *superagency* has been the

    A. additional layers of control and additional lines of command
    B. merger of departmental functions
    C. political manipulation
    D. professional incompetence in administration

22. The management of a large urban city is different in many ways from the management of other systems, particularly large business organizations.
The one of the following which does NOT exemplify these differences is:

    A. A mayor, in contrast to a manager of a large business, is often held responsible for services, etc., over which he has little authority.
    B. Top management of a large urban city must deal with a greater number of different pressures from diverse interest groups.
    C. The city government, in contrast to a large business organization, often lacks adequate management controls, and goals are often ill-defined.
    D. The multiplicity of alternatives available to city government as opposed to large businesses, are substantially greater, making decision-making haphazard.

23. The function called internal control applies to those measures taken by a government agency to protect its assets. Internal control has a role to play as an enforcer of administrative edicts as well as for purposes of asset protection.
Of the following statements relating to internal control, as described above, select the *one* usually considered to be LEAST valid.

    A. Internal control makes auditing by an external agency more difficult.
    B. The function of internal control often involves the auditing process.
    C. That people cannot be trusted to act wisely and honestly seems to be implicit in all the principles of internal control.
    D. Internal control is simply a form of self-audit by the agency itself.

24. In addition to the new effect on workers who are unskilled and undereducated, the severe effect of the high unemployment rate in the city has recently become MOST apparent among

    A. skilled craftsmen in the building trades
    B. clerical employees
    C. middle management personnel
    D. architects and engineers

25. The fact that the city has the second highest jobless rate of any major U.S. city except Detroit is considered particularly significant because, compared to Detroit, unemployment in the city   25.____

    A. is caused by city government fiscal measures rather than private business conditions
    B. exists in more than one industry
    C. results in an increase in welfare expenditures to a greater extent
    D. more seriously affects the world-wide economy

KEY (CORRECT ANSWERS)

1. D		11. D
2. D		12. D
3. A		13. A
4. A		14. A
5. C		15. B
6. A		16. B
7. D		17. C
8. A		18. A
9. C		19. D
10. A		20. C

21. A
22. D
23. A
24. A
25. B

EVALUATING CONCLUSIONS BASED ON FACTUAL INFORMATION

Test material will be presented in a multiple-choice question format.

Test Task: You will be given a set of statements and a conclusion based on the statements. You are to assume the statements are true. The conclusion is reached from these statements *only* not on what you may happen to know about the subject discussed. Each question has three possible answers. You must then select the correct answer in the following manner:

Select A, if the statements prove that the conclusion is true.
Select B, if the statements prove that the conclusion is false.
Select C, if the statements are inadequate to prove the conclusion either true or false.

SAMPLE QUESTION #1:

STATEMENTS: All uniforms are cleaned by the Conroy Company. Blue uniforms are cleaned on Mondays or Fridays; green or brown uniforms are cleaned on Wednesdays. Alan and Jean have blue uniforms, Gary has green uniforms, and Ryan has brown uniforms.

CONCLUSION: Jean's uniforms are cleaned on Wednesdays.
  A statements prove the conclusion TRUE
  B statements prove the conclusion FALSE
  C statements are INADEQUATE to prove the conclusion

The correct answer to this sample question is Choice B.

SOLUTION: The last sentence of the statements says that Jean has blue uniforms. The second sentence of the statements says that blue uniforms are cleaned on Monday or Friday. The conclusion says Jean's uniforms are cleaned on Wednesday. Wednesday is neither Monday nor Friday. Therefore, the conclusion must be false (choice B).

SAMPLE QUESTION #2

STATEMENTS: If Beth works overtime, the assignment will be completed. If the assignment is completed, then all unit employees will receive a bonus. Beth works overtime.

CONCLUSION: A bonus will be given to all employees in the unit.
  A. statements prove the conclusion TRUE.
  B. statements prove the conclusion FALSE.
  C. statements are INADEQUATE to prove the conclusion

The correct answer to this sample question is Choice A.

SOLUTION: The conclusion follows necessarily from the statements. Beth works overtime. The assignment is completed. Therefore, all unit employees will receive a bonus.

SAMPLE QUESTION #3

STATEMENTS: Bill is older than Wanda. Edna is older than Bill. Sarah is twice as old as Wanda.

CONCLUSION: Sarah is older than Edna.
- A. statements prove the conclusion TRUE
- B. statements prove the conclusion FALSE
- C. statements are INADEQUATE to prove the conclusion

The correct answer to this sample question is Choice C.

SOLUTION: We know from the statements that both Sarah and Edna are older than Wanda. We do not have any other information about Sarah and Edna. Therefore, no conclusion about whether or not Sarah is older than Edna can be made.

EVALUATING CONCLUSIONS IN LIGHT OF KNOWN FACTS
EXAMINATION SECTION
TEST 1

DIRECTIONS: Each question or incomplete statement is followed by several suggested answers or completions. Select the one that BEST answers the question or completes the statement. *PRINT THE LETTER OF THE CORRECT ANSWER IN THE SPACE AT THE RIGHT.*

Questions 1-9.

DIRECTIONS: In Questions 1 through 9, you will read a set of facts and a conclusion drawn from them. The conclusion may be valid or invalid, based on the facts—it's your task to determine the validity of the conclusion.

For each question, select the letter before the statement that BEST expresses the relationship between the given facts and the conclusion that has been drawn from them. Your choices are:
 A. The facts prove the conclusion;
 B. The facts disprove the conclusion; or
 C. The facts neither prove nor disprove the conclusion.

1. FACTS: If the supervisor retires, James, the assistant supervisor, will not be transferred to another department. James will be promoted to supervisor if he is not transferred. The supervisor retired.

    CONCLUSION: James will be promoted to supervisor.
    A. The facts prove the conclusion.
    B. The facts disprove the conclusion.
    C. The facts neither prove nor disprove the conclusion.

    1.____

2. FACTS: In the town of Luray, every player on the softball team works at Luray National Bank. In addition, every player on the Luray softball team wear glasses.

    CONCLUSIONS: At least some of the people who work at Luray National Bank wear glasses.
    A. The facts prove the conclusion.
    B. The facts disprove the conclusion.
    C. The facts neither prove nor disprove the conclusion.

    2.____

3. FACTS: The only time Henry and June go out to dinner is on an evening when they have childbirth classes. Their childbirth classes meet on Tuesdays and Thursdays.

    3.____

CONCLUSION: Henry and June never go out to dinner on Friday or Saturday.
- A. The facts prove the conclusion.
- B. The facts disprove the conclusion.
- C. The facts neither prove nor disprove the conclusion.

4. FACTS: Every player on the field hockey team has at least one bruise. Everyone on the field hockey team also has scarred knees.

   CONCLUSION: Most people with both bruises and scarred knees are field hockey players.
   - A. The facts prove the conclusion.
   - B. The facts disprove the conclusion.
   - C. The facts neither prove nor disprove the conclusion.

   4.____

5. FACTS: In the chess tournament, Lance will win his match against Jane if Jane wins her match against Mathias. If Lance wins his match against Jane, Christine will not win her match against Jane.

   CONCLUSION: Christine will not win her match against Jane if Jane wins her match against Mathias.
   - A. The facts prove the conclusion.
   - B. The facts disprove the conclusion.
   - C. The facts neither prove nor disprove the conclusion.

   5.____

6. FACTS: No green lights on the machine are indicators for the belt drive status. Not all of the lights on the machine's upper panel are green. Some lights on the machine's lower panel are green.

   CONCLUSION: The green lights on the machine's lower panel may be indicators for the belt drive status.
   - A. The facts prove the conclusion.
   - B. The facts disprove the conclusion.
   - C. The facts neither prove nor disprove the conclusion.

   6.____

7. FACTS: At a small, one-room country school, there are eight students: Amy, Ben, Carla, Dan, Elliot, Francine, Greg, and Hannah. Each student is in either the 6th, 7th, or 8th grade. Either two or three students are in each grade. Amy, Dan, and Francine are all in different grades. Ben and Elliot are both in the 7th grade. Hannah and Carl are in the same grade.

   CONCLUSION: Exactly three students are in the 7th grade.
   - A. The facts prove the conclusion.
   - B. The facts disprove the conclusion.
   - C. The facts neither prove nor disprove the conclusion.

   7.____

8. FACTS: Two married couples are having lunch together. Two of the four people are German and two are Russian, but in each couple the nationality of the spouse is not necessarily the same as the other's. One person in the group is a teacher, the other a lawyer, one an engineer, and the other a writer. The teacher is a Russian man. The writer is Russian, and her husband is an engineer. One of the people, Mr. Stern, is German.

   CONCLUSION: Mr. Stern's wife is a writer.
   A. The facts prove the conclusion.
   B. The facts disprove the conclusion.
   C. The facts neither prove nor disprove the conclusion.

   8.____

9. FACTS: The flume ride at the county fair is open only to children who are at least 36 inches tall. Lisa is 30 inches tall. John is shorter than Henry, but more than 10 inches taller than Lisa.

   CONCLUSION: Lisa is the only one who can't ride the flume ride.
   A. The facts prove the conclusion.
   B. The facts disprove the conclusion.
   C. The facts neither prove nor disprove the conclusion.

   9.____

Questions 10-17.

DIRECTIONS: Questions 10 through 17 are based on the following reading passage. It is not your knowledge of the particular topic that is being tested, but your ability to reason based on what you have read. The passage is likely to detail several proposed courses of action and factors affecting these proposals. The reading passage is followed by a conclusion or outcome based on the facts in the passage, or a description of a decision taken regarding the situation. The conclusion is followed by a number of statements that have a possible connection to the conclusion. For each statement, you are to determine whether:
   A. The statement proves the conclusion.
   B. The statement supports the conclusion but does not prove it.
   C. The statement disproves the conclusion.
   D. The statement weakens the conclusion but does not disprove it.
   E. The statement has no relevance to the conclusion.

Remember that the conclusion after the passage is to be accepted as the outcome of what actually happened, and that you are being asked to evaluate the impact each statement would have had on the conclusion.

PASSAGE:

The Grand Army of Foreign Wars, a national veteran's organization, is struggling to maintain its National Home, where the widowed spouses and orphans of deceased members are housed together in a small village-like community. The Home is open to spouses and children who are bereaved for any reason, regardless of whether the member's death was related to military service, but a new global conflict has led to a dramatic surge in the number of members' deaths: many veterans who re-enlisted for the conflict have been killed in action.

The Grand Army of Foreign Wars is considering several options for handling the increased number of applications for housing at the National Home, which has been traditionally supported by membership due. At its national convention, it will choose only one of the following:

The first idea is a one-time $50 tax on all members, above and beyond the dues they pay already. Since the organization has more than a million member, this tax should be sufficient for the construction and maintenance of new housing for applicants on the existing grounds of the National Home. The idea is opposed, however, by some older members who live on fixed incomes. These members object in principle to the taxation of Grand Army members. The Grand Army has never imposed a tax on its members.

The second idea is to launch a national fundraising drive the public relations campaign that will attract donations for the National Home. Several national celebrities are members of the organization, and other celebrities could be attracted to the cause. Many Grand Army members are wary of this approach, however: in the past, the net receipts of some fundraising efforts have been relatively insignificant, given the costs of staging them.

A third approach, suggested by many of the younger members, is to have new applicants share some of the costs of construction and maintenance. The spouses and children would pay an up-front "enrollment" fee, based on a sliding scale proportionate to their income and assets, and then a monthly fee adjusted similarly to contribute to maintenance costs. Many older members are strongly opposed to this idea, as it is in direct contradiction to the principles on which the organization was founded more than a century ago.

The fourth option is simply to maintain the status quo, focus the organization's efforts on supporting the families who already live at the National Home, and wait to accept new applicants based on attrition.

CONCLUSION: At its annual national convention, the Grand Army of Foreign Wars votes to impose a one-time tax of $10 on each member for the purpose of expanding and supporting the National Home to welcome a larger number of applicants. The tax is considered to be the solution most likely to produce the funds needed to accommodate the growing number of applicants.

10. Actuarial studies have shown that because the Grand Army's membership consists mostly of older veterans from earlier wars, the organization's membership will suffer a precipitous decline in numbers in about five years.
    A. The statement proves the conclusion.
    B. The statement supports the conclusion but does not prove it.
    C. The statement disproves the conclusion.
    D. The statement weakens the conclusion but does not disprove it.
    E. The statement has no relevance to the conclusion.

11. After passage of the funding measure, a splinter group of older members appeals for the "sliding scale" provision to be applied to the tax, so that some members may be allowed to contribute less based on their income.
    A. The statement proves the conclusion.
    B. The statement supports the conclusion but does not prove it.
    C. The statement disproves the conclusion.
    D. The statement weakens the conclusion but does not disprove it.
    E. The statement has no relevance to the conclusion.

12. The original charter of the Grand Army of Foreign Wars specifically states that the organization will not levy taxes or duties on its members beyond its modest annual dues. It takes a super-majority of attending delegates at the national convention to make alterations to the charter.
    A. The statement proves the conclusion.
    B. The statement supports the conclusion but does not prove it.
    C. The statement disproves the conclusion.
    D. The statement weakens the conclusion but does not disprove it.
    E. The statement has no relevance to the conclusion.

13. Six months before Grand Army of Foreign Wars' national convention, the Internal Revenue Service rules that because it is an organization that engages in political lobbying, the Grand Army must no longer enjoy its own federal tax-exempt status.
    A. The statement proves the conclusion.
    B. The statement supports the conclusion but does not prove it.
    C. The statement disproves the conclusion.
    D. The statement weakens the conclusion but does not disprove it.
    E. The statement has no relevance to the conclusion.

14. Two months before the national convention, Dirk Rockwell, arguably the country's most famous film actor, announces in a nationally televised interview that he has been saddened to learn of the plight of the National Home, and that he is going to make it his own personal crusade to see that it is able to house and support a greater number of widowed spouses and orphans in the future.
    A. The statement proves the conclusion.
    B. The statement supports the conclusion but does not prove it.
    C. The statement disproves the conclusion.
    D. The statement weakens the conclusion but does not disprove it.
    E. The statement has no relevance to the conclusion.

15. The Grand Army's final estimate is that the cost of expanding the National Home to accommodate the increased number of applicants will be about $61 million.
    A. The statement proves the conclusion.
    B. The statement supports the conclusion but does not prove it.
    C. The statement disproves the conclusion.
    D. The statement weakens the conclusion but does not disprove it.
    E. The statement has no relevance to the conclusion.

16. Just before the national convention, the Federal Department of Veterans Affairs announces steep cuts in the benefits package that is currently offered to the widowed spouses and orphans of veterans.
    A. The statement proves the conclusion.
    B. The statement supports the conclusion but does not prove it.
    C. The statement disproves the conclusion.
    D. The statement weakens the conclusion but does not disprove it.
    E. The statement has no relevance to the conclusion.

17. After the national convention, the Grand Army of Foreign Wars begins charging a modest "start-up" fee to all families who apply for residence at the national home.
    A. The statement proves the conclusion.
    B. The statement supports the conclusion but does not prove it.
    C. The statement disproves the conclusion.
    D. The statement weakens the conclusion but does not disprove it.
    E. The statement has no relevance to the conclusion.

17.____

Questions 18-25.

DIRECTIONS: Questions 18 through 25 each provide four factual statements and a conclusion based on these statements. After reading the entire question, you will decide whether:
    A. The conclusion is proved by statements I-IV;
    B. The conclusion is disproved by statements I-IV.
    C. The facts are not sufficient to prove or disprove the conclusion.

18. FACTUAL STATEMENTS:
    I. In the Field Day high jump competition, Martha jumped higher than Frank.
    II. Carl jumped higher than Ignacio.
    III. Ignacio jumped higher than Frank.
    IV. Dan jumped higher than Carl.

    CONCLUSION: Frank finished last in the high jump competition.
    A. The conclusion is proved by statements I-IV;
    B. The conclusion is disproved by statements I-IV.
    C. The facts are not sufficient to prove or disprove the conclusion.

18.____

19. FACTUAL STATEMENTS:
    I. The door to the hammer mill chamber is locked if light 6 is red.
    II. The door to the hammer mill chamber is locked only when the mill is operating.
    III. If the mill is not operating, light 6 is blue.
    IV. Light 6 is blue.

    CONCLUSION: The door to the hammer mill chamber is locked.
    A. The conclusion is proved by statements I-IV;
    B. The conclusion is disproved by statements I-IV.
    C. The facts are not sufficient to prove or disprove the conclusion.

19.____

20. FACTUAL STATEMENTS:
    I. Ziegfried, the lion tamer at the circus, has demanded ten additional minutes of performance time during each show.
    II. If Ziegfried is allowed his ten additional minutes per show, he will attempt to teach Kimba the tiger to shoot a basketball.
    III. If Kimba learns how to shoot a basketball, then Ziegfried was not given his ten additional minutes.
    IV. Ziegfried was given his ten additional minutes.

20.____

7 (#1)

CONCLUSION: Despite Ziegfried's efforts, Kimba did not learn how to shoot a basketball.
   A. The conclusion is proved by statements I-IV;
   B. The conclusion is disproved by statements I-IV.
   C. The facts are not sufficient to prove or disprove the conclusion.

21. FACTUAL STATEMENTS:
    I. If Stan goes to counseling, Sara won't divorce him.
    II. If Sara divorces Stan, she'll move back to Texas.
    III. If Sara doesn't divorce Stan, Irene will be disappointed.
    IV. Stan goes to counseling.

    CONCLUSION: Irene will be disappointed.
       A. The conclusion is proved by statements I-IV;
       B. The conclusion is disproved by statements I-IV.
       C. The facts are not sufficient to prove or disprove the conclusion.

21._____

22. FACTUAL STATEMENTS:
    I. If Delia is promoted to district manager, Claudia will have to be promoted to team leader.
    II. Delia will be promoted to district manager unless she misses her fourth-quarter sales quota.
    III. If Claudia is promoted to team leader, Thomas will be promoted to assistant team leader.
    IV. Delia meets her fourth-quarter sales quota.

    CONCLUSION: Thomas is promoted to assistant team leader.
       A. The conclusion is proved by statements I-IV;
       B. The conclusion is disproved by statements I-IV.
       C. The facts are not sufficient to prove or disprove the conclusion.

22._____

23. FACTUAL STATEMENTS:
    I. Clone D is identical to Clone B.
    II. Clone B is not identical to Clone A.
    III. Clone D is not identical to Clone C.
    IV. Clone E is not identical to the clones that are identical to Clone B.

    CONCLUSION: Clone E is identical to Clone D.
       A. The conclusion is proved by statements I-IV;
       B. The conclusion is disproved by statements I-IV.
       C. The facts are not sufficient to prove or disprove the conclusion.

23._____

24. FACTUAL STATEMENTS:
    I. In the Stafford Tower, each floor is occupied by a single business.
    II. Big G Staffing is on a floor between CyberGraphics and MainEvent.
    III. Gasco is on the floor directly below CyberGraphics and three floors above Treehorn Audio.
    IV. MainEvent is five floors below EZ Tax and four floors below Treehorn Audio.

24._____

CONCLUSION: EZ Tax is on a floor between Gasco and MainEvent.
  A. The conclusion is proved by statements I-IV;
  B. The conclusion is disproved by statements I-IV.
  C. The facts are not sufficient to prove or disprove the conclusion.

25. FACTUAL STATEMENTS:
  I. Only county roads lead to Nicodemus.
  II. All the roads from Hill City to Graham County are federal highways.
  III. Some of the roads from Plainville lead to Nicodemus.
  IV. Some of the roads running from Hill City lead to Strong City.

  CONCLUSION: Some of the roads from Plainville are county roads.
  A. The conclusion is proved by statements I-IV;
  B. The conclusion is disproved by statements I-IV.
  C. The facts are not sufficient to prove or disprove the conclusion.

KEY (CORRECT ANSWERS)

1.	A		11.	A
2.	A		12.	D
3.	A		13.	E
4.	C		14.	D
5.	A		15.	B
6.	B		16.	B
7.	A		17.	C
8.	A		18.	A
9.	A		19.	B
10.	E		20.	A

21.	A
22.	A
23.	B
24.	A
25.	A

SOLUTIONS TO PROBLEMS

1. CORRECT ANSWER: A
   Given Statement 3, we deduce that James will not be transferred to another department. By Statement 2, we can conclude that James will be promoted.

2. CORRECT ANSWER: A
   Since every player on the softball team wears glasses, these individuals compose some of the people who work at the bank. Although not every person who works at the bank plays softball, those bank employees who do play softball wear glasses.

3. CORRECT ANSWER: A
   If Henry and June go out to dinner, we conclude that it must be on Tuesday or Thursday, which are the only two days when they have childbirth classes. This implies that if it is not Tuesday or Thursday, then this couple does not go out to dinner.

4. CORRECT ANSWER: C
   We can only conclude that if a person plays on the field hockey team, then he or she has both bruises and scarred knees. But there are probably a great number of people who have both bruises and scarred knees but do not play on the field hockey team. The given conclusion can neither be proven or disproven.

5. CORRECT ANSWER: A
   From statement 1, if Jane beats Mathias, then Lance will beat Jane. Using statement 2, we can then conclude that Christine will not win her match against Jane.

6. CORRECT ANSWER: B
   Statement 1 tells us that no green light can be an indicator of the belt drive status. Thus, the given conclusion must be false.

7. CORRECT ANSWER: A
   We already know that Ben and Elliot are in the 7th grade. Even though Hannah and Carl are in the same grade, it cannot be the 7th grade because we would then have at least four students in this 7th grade. This would contradict the third statement, which states that either two or three students are in each grade. Since Amy, Dan, and Francine are in different grade, exactly one of them must be in the 7th grade. Thus, Ben, Elliot, and exactly one of Amy, Dan, and Francine are the three students in the 7th grade.

8. CORRECT ANSWER: A
   One man is a teacher, who is Russian. We know that the writer is female and is Russian. Since her husband is an engineer, he cannot be the Russian teacher. Thus, her husband is of German descent, namely Mr. Stern. This means that Mr. Stern's wife is the writer. Note that one couple consists of a male Russian teacher and a female German lawyer. The other couple consists of a male German engineer and a female Russian writer.

9. CORRECT ANSWER: A
Since John is more than 10 inches taller than Lisa, his height is at least 46 inches. Also, John is shorter than Henry, so Henry's height must be greater than 46 inches. Thus, Lisa is the only one whose height is less than 36 inches. Therefore, she is the only one who is not allowed on the flume ride.

18. CORRECT ANSWER: A
Dan jumped higher than Carl, who jumped higher than Ignacio, who jumped higher than Frank. Since Martha jumped higher than Frank, every person jumped higher than Frank. Thus, Frank finished last.

19. CORRECT ANSWER: B
If the light is red, then the door is locked. If the door is locked, then the mill is operating. Reversing the logical sequence of these statements, if the mill is not operating, then the door is not locked, which means that the light is blue. Thus, the given conclusion is disproved.

20. CORRECT ANSWER: A
Using the contrapositive of statement III, Ziegfried was given his ten additional minutes, then Kimba did not learn how to shoot a basketball. Since statement IV is factual, the conclusion is proved.

21. CORRECT ANSWER: A
From Statements IV and I, we conclude that Sara doesn't divorce Stan. Then statement III reveals that Irene will be disappointed. Thus, the conclusion is proved.

22. CORRECT ANSWER: A
Statement II can be rewritten as "Delia is promoted to district manager or she misses her sales quota." Furthermore, this statement is equivalent to "If Delia makes her sales quota, then she is promoted to district manager." From statement I, we conclude that Claudia is promoted to team leader. Finally, by statement III, Thomas is promoted to assistant team leader.

23. CORRECT ANSWER: B
By statement IV, Clone E is not identical to any clones identical to Clone B. Statement I tells us that Clones B and D are identical. Therefore, Clone E cannot be identical to Clone D. The conclusion is disproved.

24. CORRECT ANSWER: A
Based on all four statements, CyberGraphics is somewhere below MainEvent. Gasco is one floor below CyberGraphics. EZ Tax is two floors below Gasco. Treehorn Audio is one floor below EZ Tax. MainEvent is four floors below Treehorn Audio. Thus, EZ Tax is two floors below Gasco and five floors above MainEvent. The conclusion is proved.

25. CORRECT ANSWER: A
From statement III, we know that some of the roads from Plainville lead to Nicodemus. But statement I tells us that only county roads lead to Nicodemus. Therefore, some of the roads from Plainville must be county roads. The conclusion is proved.

TEST 2

DIRECTIONS: Each question or incomplete statement is followed by several suggested answers or completions. Select the one that BEST answers the question or completes the statement. *PRINT THE LETTER OF THE CORRECT ANSWER IN THE SPACE AT THE RIGHT.*

Questions 1-9.

DIRECTIONS: In Questions 1 through 9, you will read a set of facts and a conclusion drawn from them. The conclusion may be valid or invalid, based on the facts—it's your task to determine the validity of the conclusion.

For each question, select the letter before the statement that BEST expresses the relationship between the given facts and the conclusion that has been drawn from them. Your choices are:
    A. The facts prove the conclusion;
    B. The facts disprove the conclusion; or
    C. The facts neither prove nor disprove the conclusion.

1. FACTS: Some employees in the testing department are statisticians. Most of the statisticians who work in the testing department are projection specialists. Tom Wilks works in the testing department.

    CONCLUSION: Tom Wilks is a statistician.
        A. The facts prove the conclusion.
        B. The facts disprove the conclusion.
        C. The facts neither prove nor disprove the conclusion.

2. FACTS: Ten coins are split among Hank, Lawrence, and Gail. If Lawrence gives his coins to Hank, then Hank will have more coins than Gail. If Gail gives her coins to Lawrence, then Lawrence will have more coins than Hank.

    CONCLUSION: Hank has six coins.
        A. The facts prove the conclusion.
        B. The facts disprove the conclusion.
        C. The facts neither prove nor disprove the conclusion.

3. FACTS: Nobody loves everybody. Janet loves Ken. Ken loves everybody who loves Janet.

    CONCLUSION: Everybody loves Janet.
        A. The facts prove the conclusion.
        B. The facts disprove the conclusion.
        C. The facts neither prove nor disprove the conclusion.

4. FACTS: Most of the Torres family lives in East Los Angeles. Many people in East Los Angeles celebrate Cinco de Mayo. Joe is a member of the Torres family.

   CONCLUSION: Joe lives in East Los Angeles.
   A. The facts prove the conclusion.
   B. The facts disprove the conclusion.
   C. The facts neither prove nor disprove the conclusion.

   4._____

5. FACTS: Five professionals each occupy one story of a five-story office building. Dr. Kane's office is above Dr. Assad's. Dr. Johnson's office is between Dr. Kane's and Dr. Conlon's. Dr. Steen's office is between Dr. Conlon's and Dr. Assad's. Dr. Johnson is on the fourth story.

   CONCLUSION: Dr. Kane occupies the top story.
   A. The facts prove the conclusion.
   B. The facts disprove the conclusion.
   C. The facts neither prove nor disprove the conclusion.

   5._____

6. FACTS: To be eligible for membership in the Yukon Society, a person must be able to either tunnel through a snowbank while wearing only a T-shirt and short, or hold his breath for two minutes under water that is 50°F. Ray can only hold his breath for a minute and a half.

   CONCLUSION: Ray can still become a member of the Yukon Society by tunneling through a snowbank while wearing a T-shirt and shorts.
   A. The facts prove the conclusion.
   B. The facts disprove the conclusion.
   C. The facts neither prove nor disprove the conclusion.

   6._____

7. FACTS: A mark is worth five plunks. You can exchange four sharps for a tinplot. It takes eight marks to buy a sharp.

   CONCLUSION: A sharp is the most valuable.
   A. The facts prove the conclusion.
   B. The facts disprove the conclusion.
   C. The facts neither prove nor disprove the conclusion.

   7._____

8. FACTS: There are gibbons, as well as lemurs, who like to play in the trees at the monkey house. All those who like to play in the trees at the monkey house are fed lettuce and bananas.

   CONCLUSION: Lemurs and gibbons are types of monkeys.
   A. The facts prove the conclusion.
   B. The facts disprove the conclusion.
   C. The facts neither prove nor disprove the conclusion.

   8._____

9. FACTS: None of the Blackfoot tribes is a Salishan Indian tribe. Salishan Indians came from the northern Pacific Coast. All Salishan Indians live each of the Continental Divide.

   CONCLUSION: No Blackfoot tribes live east of the Continental Divide.
   A. The facts prove the conclusion.
   B. The facts disprove the conclusion.
   C. The facts neither prove nor disprove the conclusion.

9.____

Questions 10-17.

DIRECTIONS: Questions 10 through 17 are based on the following reading passage. It is not your knowledge of the particular topic that is being tested, but your ability to reason based on what you have read. The passage is likely to detail several proposed courses of action and factors affecting these proposals. The reading passage is followed by a conclusion or outcome based on the facts in the passage, or a description of a decision taken regarding the situation. The conclusion is followed by a number of statements that have a possible connection to the conclusion. For each statement, you are to determine whether:
   A. The statement proves the conclusion.
   B. The statement supports the conclusion but does not prove it.
   C. The statement disproves the conclusion.
   D. The statement weakens the conclusion but does not disprove it.
   E. The statement has no relevance to the conclusion.

Remember that the conclusion after the passage is to be accepted as the outcome of what actually happened, and that you are being asked to evaluate the impact each statement would have had on the conclusion.

PASSAGE:

On August 12, Beverly Willey reported that she was in the elevator late on the previous evening after leaving her office on the 16th floor of a large office building. In her report, she states that a man got on the elevator at the 11th floor, pulled her off the elevator, assaulted her, and stole her purse. Ms. Willey reported that she had seen the man in the elevators and hallways of the building before. She believes that the man works in the building. Her description of him is as follows: he is tall, unshaven, with wavy brown hair and a scar on his left cheek. He walks with a pronounced limp, often dragging his left foot behind his right.

CONCLUSION: After Beverly Willey makes her report, the police arrest a 43-year-old man, Barton Black, and charge him with her assault.

4 (#2)

10. Barton Black is a former Marine who served in Vietnam, where he sustained shrapnel wounds to the left side of his face and suffered nerve damage in his left leg.
    A. The statement proves the conclusion.
    B. The statement supports the conclusion but does not prove it.
    C. The statement disproves the conclusion.
    D. The statement weakens the conclusion but does not disprove it.
    E. The statement has no relevance to the conclusion.

    10.____

11. When they arrived at his residence to question him, detectives were greeted at the door by Barton Black, who was tall and clean-shaven.
    A. The statement proves the conclusion.
    B. The statement supports the conclusion but does not prove it.
    C. The statement disproves the conclusion.
    D. The statement weakens the conclusion but does not disprove it.
    E. The statement has no relevance to the conclusion.

    11.____

12. Barton Black was booked into the county jail several days after Beverly Willey's assault.
    A. The statement proves the conclusion.
    B. The statement supports the conclusion but does not prove it.
    C. The statement disproves the conclusion.
    D. The statement weakens the conclusion but does not disprove it.
    E. The statement has no relevance to the conclusion.

    12.____

13. Upon further investigation, detectives discover that Beverly Willey does not work at the office building.
    A. The statement proves the conclusion.
    B. The statement supports the conclusion but does not prove it.
    C. The statement disproves the conclusion.
    D. The statement weakens the conclusion but does not disprove it.
    E. The statement has no relevance to the conclusion.

    13.____

14. Upon further investigation, detectives discover that Barton Black does not work at the office building.
    A. The statement proves the conclusion.
    B. The statement supports the conclusion but does not prove it.
    C. The statement disproves the conclusion.
    D. The statement weakens the conclusion but does not disprove it.
    E. The statement has no relevance to the conclusion.

    14.____

15. In the spring of the following year, Barton Black is convicted of assaulting Beverly Willey on August 11.
    A. The statement proves the conclusion.
    B. The statement supports the conclusion but does not prove it.
    C. The statement disproves the conclusion.
    D. The statement weakens the conclusion but does not disprove it.
    E. The statement has no relevance to the conclusion.

    15.____

16. During their investigation of the assault, detectives determine that Beverly Willey was assaulted on the 12th floor of the office building.
    A. The statement proves the conclusion.
    B. The statement supports the conclusion but does not prove it.
    C. The statement disproves the conclusion.
    D. The statement weakens the conclusion but does not disprove it.
    E. The statement has no relevance to the conclusion.

17. The day after Beverly Willey's assault, Barton Black fled the area and was never seen again.
    A. The statement proves the conclusion.
    B. The statement supports the conclusion but does not prove it.
    C. The statement disproves the conclusion.
    D. The statement weakens the conclusion but does not disprove it.
    E. The statement has no relevance to the conclusion.

Questions 18-25.

DIRECTIONS: Questions 18 through 25 each provide four factual statements and a conclusion based on these statements. After reading the entire question, you will decide whether:
    A. The conclusion is proved by statements I-IV;
    B. The conclusion is disproved by statements I-IV.
    C. The facts are not sufficient to prove or disprove the conclusion.

18. FACTUAL STATEMENTS:
    I. Among five spice jars on the shelf, the sage is to the right of the parsley.
    II. The pepper is to the left of the basil.
    III. The nutmeg is between the sage and the pepper.
    IV. The pepper is the second spice from the left.

    CONCLUSION: The safe is the farthest to the right.
    A. The conclusion is proved by statements I-IV;
    B. The conclusion is disproved by statements I-IV.
    C. The facts are not sufficient to prove or disprove the conclusion.

19. FACTUAL STATEMENTS:
    I. Gear X rotates in a clockwise direction if Switch C is in the OFF position.
    II. Gear X will rotate in a counter-clockwise direction is Switch C is ON.
    III. If Gear X is rotating in a clockwise direction, then Gear Y will not be rotating at all.
    IV. Switch C is ON.

    CONCLUSION: Gear X is rotating in a counter-clockwise direction.
    A. The conclusion is proved by statements I-IV;
    B. The conclusion is disproved by statements I-IV.
    C. The facts are not sufficient to prove or disprove the conclusion.

20. FACTUAL STATEMENTS:
    I. Lane will leave for the Toronto meeting today only if Terence, Rourke, and Jackson all file their marketing reports by the end of the work day.
    II. Rourke will file her report on time only if Ganz submits last quarter's data.
    III. If Terence attends the security meeting, he will attend it with Jackson, and they will not file their marketing reports by the end of the work day.

    CONCLUSION: Lane will leave for the Toronto meeting today.
    A. The conclusion is proved by statements I-IV;
    B. The conclusion is disproved by statements I-IV.
    C. The facts are not sufficient to prove or disprove the conclusion.

21. FACTUAL STATEMENTS:
    I. Bob is in second place in the Boston Marathon.
    II. Gregory is winning the Boston Marathon.
    III. There are four miles to go in the race, and Bob is gaining on Gregory at the rate of 100 yards every minute.
    IV. There are 1760 yards in a mile and Gregory's usual pace during the Boston Marathon is one mile every six minutes.

    CONCLUSION: Bob wins the Boston Marathon.
    A. The conclusion is proved by statements I-IV;
    B. The conclusion is disproved by statements I-IV.
    C. The facts are not sufficient to prove or disprove the conclusion.

22. FACTUAL STATEMENTS:
    I. Four brothers are named Earl, John, Gary, and Pete.
    II. Earl and Pete are unmarried.
    III. John is shorter than the youngest of the four.
    IV. The oldest brother is married, and is also the tallest.

    CONCLUSION: Gary is the oldest brother.
    A. The conclusion is proved by statements I-IV;
    B. The conclusion is disproved by statements I-IV.
    C. The facts are not sufficient to prove or disprove the conclusion.

23. FACTUAL STATEMENTS:
    I. Brigade X is ten miles from the demilitarized zone.
    II. If General Woundwort gives the order, Brigade X will advance to the demilitarized zone, but not quickly enough to reach the zone before the conflict begins.
    III. Brigade Y, five miles behind Brigade X, will not advance unless General Woundwort gives the order.
    IV. Brigade Y advances.

7 (#2)

CONCLUSION: Brigade X reaches the demilitarized zone before the conflict begins.
   A. The conclusion is proved by statements I-IV;
   B. The conclusion is disproved by statements I-IV.
   C. The facts are not sufficient to prove or disprove the conclusion.

24. FACTUAL STATEMENTS: 24.____
   I. Jerry has decided to take a cab from Fullerton to Elverton.
   II. Chubby Cab charges $5 plus $3 a mile.
   III. Orange Cab charges $7.50 but gives free mileage for the first 5 miles.
   IV. After the first 5 miles, Orange Cab charges $2.50 a mile.

   CONCLUSION: Orange Cab is the cheaper fare from Fullerton to Elverton.
      A. The conclusion is proved by statements I-IV;
      B. The conclusion is disproved by statements I-IV.
      C. The facts are not sufficient to prove or disprove the conclusion.

25. FACTUAL STATEMENTS: 25.____
   I. Dan is never in class when his friend Lucy is absent.
   II. Lucy is never absent unless her mother is sick.
   III. If Lucy is in class, Sergio is in class also.
   IV. Sergio is never in class when Dalton is absent.

   CONCLUSION: If Lucy is absent, Dalton may be in class.
      A. The conclusion is proved by statements I-IV;
      B. The conclusion is disproved by statements I-IV.
      C. The facts are not sufficient to prove or disprove the conclusion.

KEY (CORRECT ANSWERS)

1.	C		11.	E
2.	B		12.	B
3.	B		13.	D
4.	C		14.	E
5.	A		15.	A
6.	A		16.	E
7.	B		17.	C
8.	C		18.	B
9.	C		19.	A
10.	B		20.	C

21.	C
22.	A
23.	B
24.	A
25.	B

SOLUTIONS TO PROBLEMS

1. **CORRECT ANSWER: C**
   Statement 1 only tells us that some employees who work in the Testing Department are statisticians. This means that we need to allow the possibility that at least one person in this department is not a statistician. Thus, if a person works in the Testing Department, we cannot conclude whether or not this individual is a statistician.

2. **CORRECT ANSWER: B**
   If Hank had six coins, then the total of Gail's collection and Lawrence's collection would be four. Thus, if Gail gave all her coins to Lawrence, Lawrence would only have four coins. Thus, it would be impossible for Lawrence to have more coins than Hank.

3. **CORRECT ANSWER: B**
   Statement 1 tells us that nobody loves everybody. If everybody loved Janet, then Statement 3 would imply that Ken loves everybody. This would contradict statement 1. The conclusion is disproved.

4. **CORRECT ANSWER: C**
   Although most of the Torres family lives in East Los Angeles, we can assume that some members of this family do not live in East Los Angeles. Thus, we cannot prove or disprove that Joe, who is a member of the Torres family, lives in East Los Angeles.

5. **CORRECT ANSWER: A**
   Since Dr. Johnson is on the 4th floor, either (a) Dr. Kane is on the 5th floor and Dr. Conlon is on the 3rd floor, or (b) Dr. Kane is on the 3rd floor and Dr. Conlon is on the 5th floor. If option (b) were correct, then since Dr. Assad would be on the 1st floor, it would be impossible for Dr. Steen's office to be between Dr. Conlon and Dr. Assad's office. Therefore, Dr. Kane's office must be on the 5th floor. The order of the doctors' offices, from 5th floor down to the 1st floor is: Dr. Kane, Dr. Johnson, Dr. Conlon, Dr. Steen, Dr. Assad.

6. **CORRECT ANSWER: A**
   Ray does not satisfy the requirement of holding his breath for two minutes under water, since he can only hold is breath for one minute in that setting. But if he tunnels through a snowbank with just a T-shirt and shorts, he will satisfy the eligibility requirement. Note that the eligibility requirement contains the key word "or." So only one of the two clauses separated by "or" need to be fulfilled.

7. **CORRECT ANSWER: B**
   Statement 2 says that four sharps is equivalent to one tinplot. This means that a tinplot is worth more than a sharp. The conclusion is disproved. We note that the order of these items, from most valuable to least valuable are: tinplot, sharp, mark, plunk.

8. **CORRECT ANSWER: C**
   We can only conclude that gibbons and lemurs are fed lettuce and bananas. We can neither prove nor disprove that these animals are types of monkeys.

9. CORRECT ANSWER: C
We know that all Salishan Indians live east of the Continental Divide. But some non-members of this tribe of Indians may also live east of the Continental Divide. Since none of the members of the Blackfoot tribe belong to the Salishan Indian tribe, we cannot draw any conclusion about the location of the Blackfoot tribe with respect to the Continental Divide.

18. CORRECT ANSWER: B
Since the pepper is second from the left and the nutmeg is between the sage and the pepper, the positions 2, 3, and 4 (from the left) are pepper, nutmeg, sage. By statement II, the basil must be in position 5, which implies that the parsley is in position 1. Therefore, the basil, not the sage, is farthest to the right. The conclusion disproved.

19. CORRECT ANSWER: A
Statement II assures us that if switch C is ON, then Gear X is rotating in a counterclockwise direction. The conclusion is proved.

20. CORRECT ANSWER: C
Based on Statement IV, followed by Statement II, we conclude that Ganz and Rourke will file their reports on time. Statement III reveals that if Terence and Jackson attend the security meeting, they will fail to file their reports on time. We have no further information if Terence and Jackson attended the security meeting, so we are not able to either confirm or deny that their reports were filed on time. This implies that we cannot know for certain that Lane will leave for his meeting in Toronto.

21. CORRECT ANSWER: C
Although Bob is in second place behind Gregory, we cannot deduce how far behind Gregory he is running. At Gregory's current pace, he will cover four miles in 24 minutes. If Bob were only 100 yards behind Gregory, he would catch up to Gregory in one minute. But if Bob were very far behind Gregory, for example 5 miles, this is the equivalent of (5)(1760) = 8800 yards. Then Bob would need 8800/100 = 88 minutes to catch up to Gregory. Thus, the given facts are not sufficient to draw a conclusion.

22. CORRECT ANSWER: A
Statement II tells us that neither Earl nor Pete could be the oldest; also, either John or Gary is married. Statement IV reveals that the oldest brother is both married and the tallest. By Statement III, John cannot be the tallest. Since John is not the tallest, he is not the oldest. Thus, the oldest brother must be Gary. The conclusion is proved.

23. CORRECT ANSWER: B
By Statements III and IV, General Woundwort must have given the order to advance. Statement II then tells us that Brigade X will advance to the demilitarized zone, but not soon enough before the conflict begins. Thus, the conclusion is disproved.

11 (#2)

24. CORRECT ANSWER: A
If the distance is 5 miles or less, then the cost for the Orange Cab is only $7.50, whereas the cost for the Chubby Cab is $5 + 3x, where x represents the number of miles traveled. For 1 to 5 miles, the cost of the Chubby Cab is between $8 and $20. This means that for a distance of 5 miles, the Orange Cab costs $7.50, whereas the Chubby Cab costs $20. After 5 miles, the cost per mile of the Chubby Cab exceeds the cost per mile of the Orange Cab. Thus, regardless of the actual distance between Fullerton and Elverton, the cost for the Orange Cab will be cheaper than that of the Chubby Cab.

25. CORRECT ANSWER: B
It looks like "Dalton" should be replaced by "Dan" in the conclusion. Then by statement I, if Lucy is absent, Dan is never in class. Thus, the conclusion is disproved.

LOGICAL REASONING
EVALUATING CONCLUSIONS IN LIGHT OF KNOWN FACTS
EXAMINATION SECTION
TEST 1

COMMENTARY

This section is designed to provide practice questions in evaluating conclusions when you are given specific data to work with.

We suggest you do the questions three at a time, consulting the answer key and then the solution section for any questions you may have missed. It's a good idea to try the questions again a week before the exam.

In the validity of conclusion type of question, you are first given a reading passage which describes a particular situation. The passage may be on any topic, as it is not your knowledge of the topic that is being tested, but your reasoning abilities. The passage is likely to detail several proposed courses of action and factors affecting these proposals. The reading passage is followed by a conclusion based on the facts in the passage, or a description of a decision taken regarding the situation. The conclusion is followed by a number of statements which have a possible connection to the conclusion. For each statement, you are to determine whether:

- A. The statement proves the conclusion.
- B. The statement supports the conclusion but does not prove it.
- C. The statement disproves the conclusion.
- D. The statement weakens the conclusion but does not disprove it.
- E. The statement has no relevance to the conclusion.

Remember that the conclusion after the passage is to be accepted as the outcome of what actually happened, and that you are being asked to evaluate the impact each statement would have had on the conclusion.

Questions 1-8.

DIRECTIONS: Questions 1 through 8 are based on the following paragraph.

In May of 2018, Mr. Bryan inherited a clothing store on Main Street in a small New England town. The store has specialized in selling quality men's and women's clothing since 1920. Business has been stable throughout the years, neither increasing nor decreasing. He has an opportunity to buy two adjacent stores which would enable him to add a wider range and style of clothing. In order to do this, he would have to borrow a substantial amount of money. He also risks losing the goodwill of his present clientele.

CONCLUSION: On November 7, 2018, Mr. Bryan tells the owner of the two adjacent stores that he has decided not to purchase them. He feels that it would be best to simply maintain his present marketing position, as there would not be enough new business to support an expansion.

A. The statement proves the conclusion.
B. The statement supports the conclusion but does not prove it.
C. The statement disproves the conclusion.
D. The statement weakens the conclusion.
E. The statement is irrelevant to the conclusion.

1. A large new branch of the county's community college holds its first classes in September.   1._____

2. The town's largest factory shuts down with no indication that it will reopen.   2._____

3. The United States Census showed that the number of children per household dropped from 2.4 to 2.1 since the last census.   3._____

4. Mr. Bryan's brother tells him of a new clothing boutique specializing in casual women's clothing which is opening soon.   4._____

5. Mr. Bryan's sister buys her baby several items for Christmas at Mr. Bryan's store.   5._____

6. Mrs. McIntyre, the President of the Town Council, brings Mr. Bryan a home-baked pumpkin pie in honor of his store's 100th anniversary. They discuss the changes that have taken place in the town, and she comments on how his store has maintained the same look and feel over the years.   6._____

7. In October, Mr. Bryan's aunt lends him $50,000.   7._____

8. The Town Council has just announced that the town is eligible for funding from a federal project designed to encourage the location of new businesses in the central districts of cities and towns.   8._____

Questions 9-18.

DIRECTIONS: Questions 9 through 18 are based on the following paragraph.

A proposal was put before the legislative body of a country to require air bags in all automobiles manufactured for domestic use in that country after 2019. The air bag, made of nylon or plastic, is designed to inflate automatically within a car at the impact of a collision, thus protecting front-seat occupants from being thrown forward. There has been much support of the measure from consumer groups, the insurance industry, key legislators, and the general public. The country's automobile manufacturers, who contend the new crash equipment would add up to $1,000 to car prices and provide no more protection than existing seat belts, are against the proposed legislation

CONCLUSION: On April 21, 2014, the legislation requiring air bags in all automobiles manufactured for domestic use in that country after 2019.

A. The statement proves the conclusion.
B. The statement supports the conclusion but does not prove it.
C. The statement disproves the conclusion.
D. The statement weakens the conclusion.
E. The statement is irrelevant to the conclusion.

9. A study has shown that 59% of car occupants do not use seat belts.   9.____

10. The country's Department of Transportation has estimated that the crash protection equipment would save up to 5,900 lives each year.   10.____

11. On April 27, 2013, Augusta Raneoni was named head of an advisory committee to gather and analyze data on the costs, benefits, and feasibility of the proposed legislation on air bags in automobiles.   11.____

12. Consumer groups and the insurance industry accuse the legislature of rejecting passage of the regulation for political reasons.   12.____

13. A study by the Committee on Imports and Exports projected that the sales of imported cars would rise dramatically in 2019 because imported cars do not have to include air bags, and can be sold more cheaply.   13.____

14. Research has shown that air bags, if produced on a large scale, would cost about $200 apiece, and would provide more reliable protection than any other type of seat belt.   14.____

15. Auto sales in 2011 increased 3% over the previous year.   15.____

16. A Department of Transportation report in July of 2020 credits a drop in automobile deaths of 4,100 to the use of air bags.   16.____

17. In June of 2014, the lobbyist of the largest insurance company receives a bonus for her work on the passage of the air bag legislation.   17.____

18. In 2020, the stock in crash protection equipment has risen three-fold over the previous year.   18.____

Questions 19-25.

DIRECTIONS: Questions 19 through 25 are based on the following paragraph.

On a national television talk show, Joan Rivera, a famous comedienne, has recently insulted the physical appearances of a famous actress and the dead wife of an ex-President. There has been a flurry of controversy over her comments, and much discussion of the incident has appeared in the press. Most of the comments have been negative. It appears that this tie she might have gone too far. There have been cancellations of two of her five scheduled performances in the two weeks since the show was televised, and Joan's been receiving a lot of negative mail. Because of the controversy, she has an interview with a national news magazine at the end of the week, and her press agent is strongly urging her to apologize publicly. She feels strongly that her comments were no worse than any other she has ever made, and that the whole incident will *blow over* soon. She respects her press agent's judgment, however, as his assessment of public sentiment tends to be very accurate.

CONCLUSION: Joan does not apologize publicly, and during the interview she challenges the actress to a weight-losing contest. For every pound the actress loses, Joan says she will donate $1 to the Cellulite Prevention League.

A. The statement proves the conclusion.
B. The statement supports the conclusion but does not prove it.
C. The statement disproves the conclusion.
D. The statement weakens the conclusion.
E. The statement is irrelevant to the conclusion.

19. Joan's mother, who she is very fond of, is very upset with Joan's comments. 19.____

20. Six months after the interview, Joan's income has doubled. 20.____

21. Joan's agent is pleased with the way Joan handles the interview. 21.____

22. Joan's sister has been appointed Treasurer of the Cellulite Prevention League 22.____
In her report, she states that Joan's $12 contribution is the only amount that
has been donated to the League in its first six months.

23. The magazine receives many letters commending Joan for the courage it 23.____
took for her to apologize publicly in the interview.

24. Immediately after the interview appears, another one of Joan's performances 24.____
is cancelled.

25. Due to a printers' strike, the article was not published until the following week. 25.____

Questions 26-30.

DIRECTIONS: Questions 25 through 30 are based on the following paragraph.

The law-making body of Country X must decide what to do about the issue of recording television shows for home use. There is currently no law against recording shows directly from the TV as long as the DVDs are not used for commercial purposes. The increasing popularity of pay TV and satellite systems, combined with the increasing number of homes that own recording equipment, has caused a great deal of concern in some segments of the entertainment industry. Companies that own the rights to films, popular television shows, and sporting events feel that their copyright privileges are being violated, and they are seeking compensation or the banning of TV recording. Legislation has been introduced to make it illegal to record television programs for home use. Separate proposed legislation is also pending that would continue to allow recording of TV shows for home use, but would place a tax of 10% on each DVD that is purchased for home use. The income from that tax would then be proportionately distributed as royalties to those owning the rights to programs being aired. A weighted point system coupled with the averaging of several national viewing rating systems would be used to determine the royalties. There is a great deal of lobbying being done for both bills, as the manufacturers of DVDs and recording equipment are against the passage of the bills.

CONCLUSION: The legislature of Country X rejects both bills by a wide margin.

A. The statement proves the conclusion.
B. The statement supports the conclusion but does not prove it.
C. The statement disproves the conclusion.
D. The statement weakens the conclusion.
E. The statement is irrelevant to the conclusion.

26. Country X's Department of Taxation hires 500 new employees to handle the increased paperwork created by the new tax on DVDs. 26.____

27. A study conducted by the country's most prestigious accounting firm shows that the cost of implementing the proposed new DVD tax would be greater than the income expected from it. 27.____

28. It is estimated that 80% of all those working in the entertainment industry, excluding performers, own DVD recorders. 28.____

29. The head of Country X's law enforcement agency states that legislation banning the home recording of TV shows would be unenforceable. 29.____

30. Financial experts predict that unless a tax is placed on DVDs, several large companies in the entertainment industry will have to file for bankruptcy. 30.____

Questions 31-38.

DIRECTIONS: Questions 31 through 38 are variations on the type of question you just had. It is important that you read the question very carefully to determine exactly what is required.

31. In this question, select the choice that is MOST relevant to the conclusion. 31.____
    I. The Buffalo Bills football team is in second place in its division.
    II. The New England Patriots are in first place in the same division.
    III. There are two games left to play in the season, and the Bills will not play the Patriots again.
    IV. The New England Patriots won ten games and lost four games, and the Buffalo Bills have won eight games and lost six games.
    CONCLUSION: The Buffalo Bills win their division.
    A. The conclusion is proved by sentences I-IV.
    B. The conclusion is disproved by sentences I-IV.
    C. The facts are not sufficient to prove or disprove the conclusion.

32. In this question, select the choice that is MOST relevant to the conclusion.   32.____
    I. On the planet of Zeinon there are only two different eye colors and only two different hair colors.
    II. Half of those beings with purple hair have golden eyes.
    III. There are more inhabitants with purple hair than there are inhabitants with silver hair.
    IV. One-third of those with silver hair have green eyes.
    CONCLUSION: There are more golden-eyed beings on Zeinon than green-eyed ones.
       A. The conclusion is proved by sentences I-IV.
       B. The conclusion is disproved by sentences I-IV.
       C. The facts are not sufficient to prove or disprove the conclusion.

33. In this question, select the choice that is MOST relevant to the conclusion.   33.____
    John and Kevin are leaving Amaranth to go to school in Bethany. They've decided to rent a small truck to move their possessions. Joe's Truck Rental charges $100 plus 30¢ a mile. National Movers charges $50 more but gives free mileage for the first 100 miles. After the first 100 miles, they charge 25¢ a mile.
    CONCLUSION: John and Kevin rent their truck from National Movers because it is cheaper.
       A. The conclusion is proved by the facts in the above paragraph.
       B. The conclusion is disproved by the facts in the above paragraph.
       C. The facts are not sufficient to prove or disprove the conclusion.

34. For this question, select the choice that supports the information given in the passage.   34.____

    Municipalities in Country X are divided into villages, towns, and cities. A village has a population of 5,000 or less. The population of a town ranges from 5,001 to 15,000. In order to be incorporated as a city, the municipality must have a population over 15,000. If, after a village becomes a town, or a town becomes a city, the population drops below the minimum required (for example, the population of a city goes below 15,000), and stays below the minimum for more than ten years, it loses its current status, and drops to the next category. As soon as a municipality rises in population to the next category (village to town, for example), however, it is immediately reclassified to the next category.

    In the 2000 census, Plainfield had a population of 12,000. Between 2000 and 2010, Plainfield grew 10%, and between 2010 and 2020 Plainfield grew another 20%. The population of Springdale doubled from 2000 to 2010, and increased 25% from 2010 to 2020. The city of Smallville's population, 20,283, has not changed significantly in recent years. Granton had a population of 25,000 people in 1990, and has decreased 25% in each ten year period since then. Ellenville had a population of 4,283 in 1990, and grew 5% in each ten year period since 1990.

In 2020,
- A. Plainfield, Smallville, and Granton are cities.
- B. Smallville is a city, Granton is a town, and Ellenville is a village.
- C. Springdale, Granton, and Ellenville are towns.
- D. Plainfield and Smallville are cities, and Ellenville is a town.

35. For this question, select the choice that is MOST relevant to the conclusion.
    A study was done for a major food-distributing firm to determine if there is any difference in the kind of caffeine containing products used by people of different ages. A sample of one thousand people between the ages of twenty and fifty were drawn from selected areas in the country. They were divided equally into three groups.
    Those individuals who were 20-29 were designated Group A, those 30-39 were Group B, and those 40-50 were placed in Group C.
    It was found that on the average, Group A drank 1.8 cups of coffee, Group B 3.1, and Group C 2.5 cups of coffee daily. Group A drank 2.1 cups of tea, Group B drank 1.2, and Group C drank 2.6 cups of tea daily. Group A drank 3 1.8 ounces glasses of cola, Group B drank 1.9, and Group C drank 1.5 glasses of cola daily.
    CONCLUSION: According to the study, the average person in the 20-29 age group drinks less tea daily than the average person in the 40-50 age group, but drinks more coffee daily than the average person in the 30-39 age group drinks cola.
    - A. The conclusion is proved by the facts in the above paragraph.
    - B. The conclusion is disproved by the facts in the above paragraph.
    - C. The facts are not sufficient to prove or disprove the conclusion.

36. For this question, select the choice that is MOST relevant to the conclusion
    - I. Mary is taller than Jane but shorter than Dale.
    - II. Fred is taller than Mary but shorter than Steven.
    - III. Dale is shorter than Steven but taller than Elizabeth.
    - IV. Elizabeth is taller than Mary but not as tall as Fred.
    CONCLUSION: Dale is taller than Fred.
    - A. The conclusion is proved by sentences I-IV.
    - B. The conclusion is disproved by sentences I-IV.
    - C. The facts are not sufficient to prove or disprove the conclusion.

37. For this question, select the choice that is MOST relevant to the conclusion.
    - I. Main Street is between Spring Street and Glenn Blvd.
    - II. Hawley Avenue is one block south of Spring Street and three blocks north of Main Street.
    - III. Glenn Street is five blocks south of Elm and four blocks south of Main.
    - IV. All the streets mentioned are parallel to one another.
    CONCLUSION: Elm Street is between Hawley Avenue and Glenn Blvd.
    - A. The conclusion is proved by the facts in sentences I-IV.
    - B. The conclusion is disproved by the facts in sentences I-IV.
    - C. The facts are not sufficient to prove or disprove the conclusion.

38. For this question, select the choice that is MOST relevant to the conclusion. 38._____
   I. Train A leaves the town of Hampshire every day at 5:50 A.M. and arrives in New London at 6:42 A.M.
   II. Train A leaves New London at 7:00 A.M. and arrives in Kellogsville at 8:42 A.M.
   III. Train B leaves Kellogsville at 8:00 A.M. and arrives in Hampshire at 10:45 A.M.
   IV. Due to the need for repairs, there is just one railroad track between New London and Hampshire.
   CONCLUSION: It is impossible for Train A and Train B to follow these schedules without colliding.
   A. The conclusion is proved by the facts in sentences I-IV.
   B. The conclusion is disproved by the facts in sentences I-IV.
   C. The facts are not sufficient to prove or disprove the conclusion.

KEY (CORRECT ANSWERS)

1.	D	11.	C	21.	D	31.	C
2.	B	12.	C	22.	A	32.	A
3.	E	13.	D	23.	C	33.	C
4.	B	14.	B	24.	B	34.	B
5.	C	15.	E	25.	E	35.	B
6.	A	16.	B	26.	C	36.	C
7.	D	17.	A	27.	B	37.	A
8.	B	18.	B	28.	E	38.	B
9.	B	19.	D	29.	B		
10.	B	20.	E	30.	D		

SOLUTIONS TO QUESTIONS

1. The answer is D. This statement weakens the conclusion, but does not disprove it. If a new branch of the community college opened in September, it could possibly bring in new business for Mr. Bryant. Since it states in the conclusion that Mr. Bryant felt there would not be enough new business to support the additional stores, this would tend to disprove the conclusion. Choice C would not be correct because it's possible that he felt that the students would not have enough additional money to support his new venture, or would not be interested in his clothing styles. It's also possible that the majority of the students already live in the area, so that they wouldn't really be a new customer population. This type of question is tricky, and can initially be very confusing, so don't feel badly if you missed it. Most people need to practice with a few of these types of questions before they feel comfortable recognizing exactly what they're being asked to do.

2. The answer is B. It supports the conclusion because the closing of the factory would probably take money and customers out of the town, causing Mr. Bryant to lose some of his present business. It doesn't prove the conclusion, however, because we don't know how large the factory was. It's possible that only a small percentage of the population was employed there, or that they found other jobs.

3. The answer is E. The fact that the number of children per household dropped slightly nationwide in the decade is irrelevant. Statistics showing a drop nationwide doesn't mean that there was a drop in the number of children per household in Mr. Bryant's hometown. This is a tricky question, as choice B, supporting the conclusion but not proving it, may seem reasonable. If the number of children per household declined nationwide, then it may not seem unreasonable to feel that this would support Mr. Bryant's decision not to expand his business. However, we're preparing you for promotional exams, not "real life." One of the difficult things about taking exams is that sometimes you're forced to make a choice between two statements that both seem like they could be the possible answer. What you need to do in that case is choose the best choice. Becoming annoyed or frustrated with the question won't really help much. If there's a review of the exam, you can certainly appeal the question. There have been many cases where, after an appeal, two possible choices have been allowed as correct answers. We've included this question, however, to help you see what to do should you get a question like this. It's most important not to get rattled, and to select the BEST choice. In this case, the connection between the statistical information and Mr. Bryant's decision is pretty remote. If the question had said that the number of children in Mr. Bryant's <u>town</u> had decreased, then choice B would have been a more reasonable choice. It could also help in this situation to visualize the situation. Picture Mr. Bryant in his armchair reading that, nationwide, the average number of children per household has declined slightly. How likely would this be to influence his decision, especially since he sells men's and women's clothing? It would take a while for this decline in population to show up, and we're not even sure if it applies to Mr. Bryant's hometown. Don't feel badly if you missed this; it was tricky. The more of these you do, the more comfortable you'll feel.

4. The answer is B. If a new clothing boutique specializing in casual women's clothing were to open soon, this would lend support to Mr. Bryant's decision not to expand, but would not prove that he had actually made the decision to expand. A new women's clothing boutique would most likely be in competition with his existing business, thus making any possible expansion a riskier venture. We can't be sure from this, however, that he didn't go ahead and expand his business despite the increased competition. Choice A, proves the conclusion, would only be the answer if we could be absolutely sure from the statement that Mr. Bryant had actually not expanded his business.

5. The answer is C. This statement disproves the conclusion. In order for his sister to buy several items for her baby at Mr. Bryant's store, he would have to have changed his business to include children's clothing.

6. The answer is A. It definitely proves the conclusion. The passage states that Mr. Bryan's store had been in business since 1920. A pie baked in honor of his store's 100th anniversary would have to be presented sometime in 2020. The conclusion states that he made his decision not to expand on November 7, 2018. If, more than a year later Mrs. MacIntyre comments that his store has maintained the same look and feel over the years, it could not have been expanded, or otherwise significantly changed.

7. The answer is D. If Mr. Bryant's aunt lent him $50,000 in October, this would tend to weaken the conclusion, which took place in November. Because it was stated that Mr. Bryant would need to borrow money in order to expand his business, it would be logical to assume that if he borrowed money he had decided to expand his business, weakening the conclusion. The reason C, disproves the conclusion, is not the correct answer is because we can't be sure Mr. Bryant didn't borrow the money for another reason.

8. The answer is B. If Mr. Bryant's town is eligible for federal funds to encourage the location of new businesses in the central district, this would tend to support his decision not to expand his business. Funds to encourage new business would increase the likelihood of there being additional competition for Mr. Bryant's store to contend with. Since we can't say for sure that there would be direct competition from a new business, however, choice A would be incorrect. Note that this is also a tricky question. You might have thought that the new funds weakened the conclusion because it would mean that Mr. Bryant could easily get the money he needed. Mr. Bryant is expanding his present business, not creating a new business. Therefore, he is not eligible for the funding.

9. The answer is B. This is a very tricky question. It's stated that 59% of car occupants don't use seat belts. The legislature is considering the use of air bags because of safety issues. The advantage of air bags over seat belts is that they inflate upon impact, and don't require car occupants to do anything with them ahead of time. Since the population has strongly resisted using seat belts, the air bags could become even more important in saving lives. Since saving lives is the purpose of the proposed legislation, the information that a small percentage of people use seat belts could be helpful to the passage of the legislation. We can't be sure that this is reason enough for the legislature to vote for the legislation, however, so choice A in incorrect.

10. The answer is B, as the information that 5,900 lives could be saved would tend to support the conclusion. Saving that many lives through the use of air bags could be a very persuasive reason to vote for the legislation. Since we don't know for sure that it's enough of a compelling reason for the legislature to vote for the legislation, however, choice A could not be the answer.

11. The answer is C, disproves the conclusion. If the legislation had been passed as stated in the conclusion, there would be no reason to appoint someone head of an advisory committee six days later to analyze the "feasibility of the proposed legislation." The key word here is "proposed." If it has been proposed, it means it hasn't been passed. This contradicts the conclusion and, therefore, disproves it.

12. The answer is C, disproves the conclusion. If the legislation had passed, there would be no reason for supporters of the legislation to accuse the legislature of rejecting the legislation for political reasons. This question may have seemed so obvious that you might have thought there was a trick to it. Exams usually have a few obvious questions, which will trip you up if you begin reading too much into them.

13. The answer is D, as this would tend to disprove the conclusion. A projected dramatic rise in imported cars could be very harmful to the country's economy and could be a very good reason for some legislators to vote against the proposed legislation. It would be assuming too much to choose C, however, because we don't know if they actually did vote against it.

14. The answer is B. This information would tend to support the passage of the legislation. The estimate of the cost of the air bags is $800 less than the cost estimated by opponents, and it's stated that the protection would be more reliable than any other type of seat belt. Both of these would be good arguments in favor of passing the legislation. Since we don't know for sure, however, how persuasive they actually were, choice A would not be the correct choice.

15. The answer is E, as this is irrelevant information. It really doesn't matter whether auto sales in 2001 have increased slightly over the previous year. If the air bag legislation were to go into effect in 2004, that might make the information somehow more relevant. But the air bag legislation would not take effect until 2009, so the information is irrelevant, since it tells us nothing about the state of the auto industry then.

16. The answer is B, supports the conclusion. This is a tricky question. While at first it might seem to prove the conclusion, we can't be sure that the air bag legislation is responsible for the drop in automobile deaths. It's possible air bags came into popular use without the legislation, or with different legislation. There's no way we can be sure that it was the proposed legislation mandating the use of air bags that was responsible.

17. The answer is A. If, in June of 2009, the lobbyist received a bonus "for her work on the air bag legislation," we can be sure that the legislation passed. This proves the conclusion.

18. The answer is B. This is another tricky question. A three-fold stock increase would strongly suggest that the legislation had been passed, but it's possible that factors other than the air bag legislation caused the increase. Note that the stock is in "crash protection

equipment." Nowhere in the statement does it say air bags. Seat belts, motorcycle helmets, and collapsible bumpers are all crash protection equipment and could have contributed to the increase. This is just another reminder to read carefully because the questions are often designed to mislead you.

19. The answer is D. This would tend to weaken the conclusion because Joan is very fond of her mother and she would not want to upset her unnecessarily. It does not prove it, however, because if Joan strongly feels she is right, she probably wouldn't let her mother's opinion sway her. Choice E would also not be correct, because we cannot assume that Joan's mother's opinion is of so little importance to her as to be considered irrelevant.

20. The answer is E. The statement is irrelevant. We are told that Joan's income has doubled but we are not old why. The phrase "six months after the interview" can be misleading in that it leads us to assume that the increase and the interview are related. Her income could have doubled because she regained her popularity but it could also have come from stocks or some other business venture. Because we are not given any reason for her income doubling, it would be impossible to say whether or not this statement proves or disproves the conclusion. Choice E is the best choice of the five possible choices. One of the problems with promotional exams is that sometimes you need to select a choice you're not crazy about. In this case, "not having enough information to made a determination" would be the best choice. However, that's not an option, so you're forced to work with what you've got. On these exams it's sometimes like voting for President; you have to pick the "lesser of the two evils" or the least awful choice. In this case, the information is more irrelevant to the conclusion than it is anything else.

21. The answer is D, weakens the conclusion. We've been told that Joan's agent feels that she should apologize. If he is pleased with her interview, then it would tend to weaken the conclusion but not disprove it. We can't be sure that he hasn't had a change of heart, or that there weren't other parts of the interview he liked so much that they outweighed her unwillingness to apologize.

22. The answer is A. The conclusion states that Joan will donate $1 to the Cellulite Prevention League for every pound the actress loses. Joan's sister's financial report on the League's activities directly supports and proves the conclusion.

23. The answer is C, disproves the conclusion. If the magazine receives many letters commending Joan for her courage in apologizing, this directly contradicts the conclusion, which states that Joan didn't apologize.

24. The answer is B. It was stated in the passage that two of Joan's performances were cancelled after the controversy first occurred. The cancellation of another performance immediately after her interview was published would tend to support the conclusion that she refused to apologize. Because we can't be sure, however, that her performance wasn't cancelled for another reason, choice A would be incorrect.

25. The answer is E, as this information is irrelevant. Postponing the article an extra week does not affect Joan's decision or the public's reaction to it.

13 (#1)

26. The answer is C. If 500 new employees are hired to handle the "increased paperwork created by the new tax on DVDs," this would directly contradict the conclusion, which states that the legislature defeated both bills. (They should all be this easy.)

27. The answer is B. The results of the study would support the conclusion. If implementing the legislation was going to be so costly, it is likely that the legislature would vote against it. Choice A is not the answer, however, because we can't be sure that the legislature didn't pass it anyway.

28. The answer is E. It's irrelevant to the conclusion that 80% of all those working in the entertainment industry own DVD recorders. Sometimes if you're not sure about these, it can help a lot to try and visualize the situation. Why would someone voting on this legislation care about this fact? It doesn't seem to be the kind of information that would make any difference or impact upon the conclusion.

29. The answer is B. The head of the law enforcement agency's statement that the legislation would be unenforceable would support the conclusion. It's possible that many legislators would question why they should bother to pass legislation that would be impossible to enforce. Choice A would be incorrect, however, because we can't be sure that the legislation wasn't passed in spite of his statement.

30. The answer is D. This would tend to weaken the conclusion because the prospect of several large companies going bankrupt would seem to be a good argument in favor of the legislation. The possible loss of jobs and businesses would be a good reason for some people to vote for the legislation. We can't be sure, however, that this would be a competing enough reason to ensure passage of the legislation so choice C is incorrect.

This concludes our section on the "Validity of Conclusion" type of questions. We hope these weren't too horrible for you. It's important to keep in mind exactly what you've been given and exactly what they want you to do with it. It's also necessary to remember that you may have to choose between two possible answers. In that case, you must choose the one that seems the best. Sometimes you may think there is no good answer. You will probably be right, but you can't let that upset you. Just choose the one you dislike the least.

We want to repeat that it is unlikely that this exact format will appear on the exam. The skills required to answer these questions, however, are the same as those you'll need for the exam so we suggest that you review this section before taking the actual exam.

31. The answer is C. This next set of questions requires you to "switch gears" slightly, and get used to different formats. In this type of question, you have to decide whether the conclusion is proved by the facts give, disproved by the facts given, or neither because note enough information has been provided. Fortunately, unlike the previous questions, you don't have to decide whether particular facts support or don't support the conclusion. This type of question is more straight forward, but the reasoning behind it is the same. We are told that the Bills have won two games less than the Patriots, and that the Patriots are in first place and the Bills are in second place. We are also told that there are two games left to play, and that they won't play each other again. The conclusion states that the Bills won the division. Is there anything in the four statements that would prove this? We have

14 (#1)

no idea what the outcome of the last two games of the season was. The Bills and Patriots could have ended up tied at the end of the season, or the Bills could have lost both or one of their last games while the Patriots did the same. There might even be another team tied for first or second place with the Bills or Patriots. Since we don't know for sure, Choice A is incorrect. Choice B is trickier. It might seem at first glance that the best the Bills could do would be to tie the Patriots if the Patriots lost their last two games and the Bills won their last two games. But it would be too much to assume that there is no procedure for a tiebreaker that wouldn't give the Bills the division championship. Since we don't know what the rules are in the event of a tie (for example, what if a tie was decided on the results of what happened when the two teams had played each other, or on the best record in the division, or on most points scored?), we can't say for sure that it would be impossible for the Bills to win their division. For this reason, choice C is the answer, as we don't have enough information to prove or disprove the conclusion. This question looked more difficult than it actually was. It's important to disregard any factors outside of the actual question, and to focus only on what you've been given. In this case, as on all of these types of questions, what you know or don't know about a subject is actually irrelevant. It's best to concentrate only on the actual facts given.

32. The answer is A. The conclusion is proved by the facts given.

   In this type of problem, it is usually best to pull as many facts as possible from the sentences and then put them into a simpler form. The phrasing and the order of exam questions are designed to be confusing so you need to restate things as clearly as possible by eliminating the extras.

   Sentence I tells us that there are only two possible colors for eyes and two for hair. Looking at the other sentences we learn that eyes are either green or gold and that hair is either silver or purple. If half the beings with purple hair have golden eyes, then the other half must have green eyes since it is the only other eye color. Likewise, if one-third of those with silver hair have green eyes, the other two-thirds must have golden eyes.

   This information makes it clear that there are more golden-eyed beings on Zeinon than green-eyed ones. It doesn't matter that we don't know exactly how many are actually living on the planet. The number of those with gold eyes (1/2 plus 2/3) will always be greater than the number of those with green eyes (1/2 plus 1/3), no matter what the actual figures might be. Sentence III is totally irrelevant because even if there were more silver-haired inhabitants it would not affect the conclusion.

33. The answer is C. The conclusion is neither proved nor disproved by the facts because we don't know how many miles Bethany is from Amoranth.

   With this type of question, if you're not sure how to approach it, you can always substitute in a range of "real numbers" to see what the result would be. If they were 200 miles apart, Joe's Truck Rental would be cheaper because they would charge a total of $160 while National Movers would charge $175.

   Joe's - $100 plus .30 x 200 (or $60) = $160
   National - $150 plus .25 x 100 (or $25) = $175

   If the towns were 600 miles apart, however, National Movers would be cheaper. The cost of renting from National would be $275 compared to the $280 charged by Joe's Trucking.

   Joe's - $100 plus .30 x 600 (or $180) = $280
   National - $150 plus .25 x 500 (or $125) = $275

15 (#1)

34. The answer is B. We've varied the format once more, but the reasoning is similar. This is a tedious question that is more like a math question, but we wanted to give you some practice with this type, just in case. You won't be able to do this question if you've forgotten how to do percents. Many exams require this knowledge, so if you feel you need a review we suggest you read Booklets 1, 2 or 3 in this series.

The only way to attack this problem is to go through each choice until you find the one that is correct. Choice A states that Plainfield, Smallville, and Granton are cities. Let's begin with Plainfield. The passage states that in 1990 Plainfield had a population of 12,000, and that it grew 10% between 1990 and 2000, and another 20% between 2000 and 2010. Ten percent of 12,000 is 1200 (12,000 x .10 = 1200). Therefore, the population grew from 12,000 in 1990 to 12,000 + 1200 between 1990 and 2000. At the time of the 2000 Census, Plainfield's population was 13,200. It then grew another 20% between 2000 and 2010, so, 13,200 x .20 = 2640. 13,200 plus the additional increase of 2640 would make the population of Plainfield 15,840. This would qualify it as a city, since its population is over 15,000. Since a change upward in the population of a municipality is re-classified immediately, Plainfield would have become a city right away. So far, statement A is true. The passage states that Smallville's population has not changed significantly in the last twenty years. Since Smallville's population was 20,283, Smallville would still be a city. Granton had a population of 25,000 (what a coincidence that so any of these places have such nice, even numbers) in 1980. The population has decreased 25% in each ten year period since that time. So from 1980 to 1990, the population decreased 25%. 25,000 x .25 = 6,250. 25,000 minus 6,250 = 18,750. So the population of Granton in 1990 would have been 18,750. (Or, you could have saved a step and multiplied 25,000 by .75 to get 18,750.) The population from 1990 to 2000 decreased an additional 25%. So: 18,750 x .25 = 4,687.50. 18,750 minus 4,687.50 = 14,062.50. Or: 18,750 x .75 = 14,062.50. (Don't let the fact that a half of a person is involved confuse you; these are exam questions, not real life.) From 2000 to 2010 the population decreased an additional 25%. This would mean that Granton's population was below 15,000 for more than ten years, so it's status as a city would have changed to that of a town, which would make choice A incorrect.

Choice B states that Smallville is a city and Granton is a town, which we know to be true from the information above. Choice B is correct so far. We next need to determine if Ellenville is a village. Ellenville had a population of 4,283 in 1980, and increased 5% in each ten year period since 1980. 4,283 x .05 = 214.15. 4,283 plus 214.15 = 4,497.15, so Ellenville's population from 1980 to 1990 increased to 4,497.15. (Or: 4,283 x 1.05 = 4,497.15.) From 1990 to 2000 Ellenville's population increased another 5%: 4,497.15 x .05 = 224.86. 4,497.15 plus 224.86 = 4,772.01 (or: 4,497.15 x 1.05 = 4,722.01.) From 2000 to 2010, Ellenville's population increased another 5%: 4,722.01 x .05 = 236.10. 4,722.01 plus 236.10 = 4,958.11. (Or: 4,722.01 x 1.05 = 4,958.11.).

Ellenville's population is still under 5,000 in 2010, so it would continue to be classified as a village. Since all three statements in choice B are true, choice B must be the answer. However, we'll go through the other choices. Choice C states that Springdale is a town. The passage tells us that the population of Springdale doubled from 1990 to 2000, and increased 25% from 2000 to 2010. It doesn't give us any actual population figures, however, so it's impossible to know what the population of Springdale is, making choice C incorrect. Choice C also states that Granton is a town, which is true, and that Ellenville is a town, which is false (from choice B we know it's a village). Choice D states that Plainfield and Smallville are cities, which is information we already know is true, and that Ellenville is a town. Since Ellenville is a village, choice D is also incorrect.

This was a lot of work for just one question and we doubt you'll get one like this on this section of the exam, but we included it just in case. On an exam, you can always put a check mark next to a question like this and come back to it later, if you feel you're pressed for time and cold spend your time more productively on other, less time-consuming problems.

35. The answer is B. This question requires very careful reading. It's best to break the conclusion down into smaller parts in order to solve the problem. The first half of the conclusion states that the average person in the 20-29 age group (Group A) drinks less tea daily than the average person in the 40-50 age group (Group C). The average person in Group A drinks 2.1 cups of tea daily, while the average person in Group C drinks 2.6 cups of tea daily. Since 2.1 is less than 2.6, the conclusion is correct so far. The second half of the conclusion states that the average person in Group A drinks more coffee daily than the average person in the 30-39 age group (Group B) drinks cola. The average person in Group A drinks 1.8 cups of coffee daily, while the average person in Group B drinks 1.9 glasses of cola. This disproves the conclusion, which states that the average person in Group A drinks more coffee daily than the average person in Group B drinks cola.

36. The answer is C. The easiest way to approach a problem that deals with the relationship between a number of different people or things is to set up a diagram. This type of problem is usually too confusing to do in your head. For this particular problem, the "diagram" could be a line, one end of which would be labeled tall and the other end labeled short. Then, taking one sentence at a time, place the people on the line to see where they fall in relation to one another.

The diagram of the first sentence would look like this:

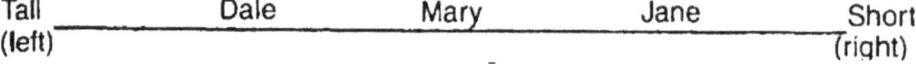

Mary is taller than Jane but shorter than Dale, so she would fall somewhere between the two of them. We have placed tall on the left and labeled it left just to make the explanation easier. You could just as easily have reversed the position.

The second sentence places Fred somewhere to the left of Mary because he is taller than she is. Steven would be to the left of Fred for the same reason. At this point we don't know whether Steven and Fred are taller or shorter than Dale. The new diagram would look like this:

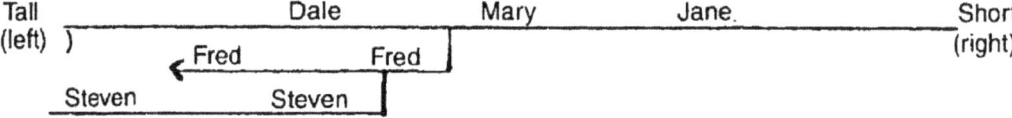

The third sentence introduces Elizabeth, presenting a new problem. Elizabeth can be anywhere to the right of Dale. Don't make the mistake of assuming she falls between Dale and Mary. At this point we don't know where she fits in relation to Mary, Jane, or even Fred.

We do get information about Steven, however. He is taller than Dale so he would be to the left of Dale. Since he is also taller than Fred (see sentence II), we know that Steven is the tallest person thus far. The diagram would now look like this:

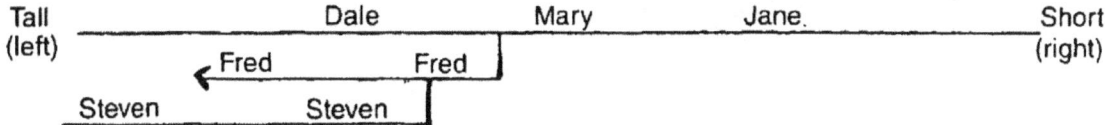

Fred's height is somewhere between Steven and Mary, Elizabeth's anywhere between Dale and the end of the line.

The fourth sentence tells us where Elizabeth stands, in relation to Fred and the others in the problem. The fact that she is taller than Mary means she is also taller than Jane. The final diagram would look like this:

| Tall (left) | Steven | Dale | Elizabeth | Mary | Jane | Short (right) |

Fred between Dale and Elizabeth.

We still don't know whether Dale or Fred is taller, however. Therefore, the conclusion that Dale is taller than Fred can't be proved. It also can't be disproved because we don't know for sure that he isn't. The answer has to be choice C, as the conclusion can't be proved or disproved.

37. The answer is A. This is another problem that is easiest for most people if they make a diagram. Sentence I states that Main Street is between Spring Street and Glenn Blvd. At this point we don't know if they are next to each other or if they are separated by a number of streets. Therefore, you should leave space between streets as you plot your first diagram.

The order of the streets could go either:

Spring St.	or	Glenn Blvd.
Main St.		Main St.
Glenn Blvd.		Spring St.

Sentence II states that Hawley Street is one block south of Spring Street and 3 blocks north of Main Street. Because most people think in terms of north as above and south as below and because it was stated that Hawley is one block south of Spring Street and three blocks north of Main Street, the next diagram could look like this:

18 (#1)

<u>Spring</u>
<u>Hawley</u>

———
———

<u>Main</u>
<u>Glenn</u>

The third sentence states that Glenn Street is five blocks south of Elm and four blocks south of Main. It could look like this:

<u>Spring</u>
<u>Hawley</u>

———

<u>Elm</u>
<u>Main</u>

———
———

<u>Glenn</u>

The conclusion states that Elm Street is between Hawley Avenue and Glenn Blvd. From the above diagram, we can see that this is the case.

38. The answer is B. For most people, the best way to do this problem is to draw a diagram, plotting the course of both trains. Sentence I states that Train A leaves Hampshire at 5:50 A.M. and reaches New London at 6:42. Your first diagram might look like this:

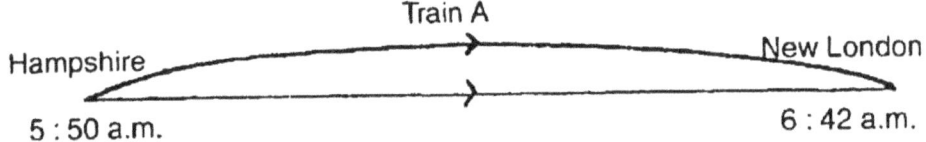

Sentence II states that the train leaves New London at 7:00 a.m. and arrives in Kellogsville at 8:42 a.m. The diagram might now look like this:

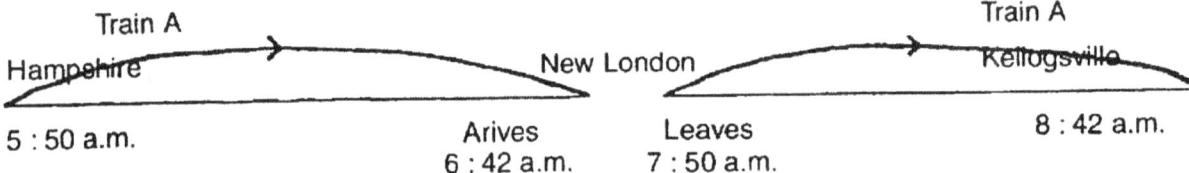

Sentence III gives us the rest of the information that must be included in the diagram. It introduces Train B, which moves in the opposite direction, leaving Kellogsville at 8:00 a.m. and arriving at Hampshire at 10:42 a.m. The final diagram might look like this:

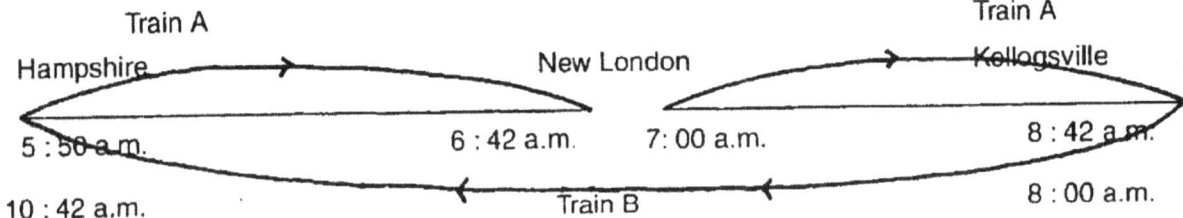

19 (#1)

As you can see from the diagram, the routes of the two trains will overlap somewhere between Kellogsville and New London. If you read sentence IV quickly and assumed that that was the section with only one track, you probably would have assumed that there would have had to be a collision. Sentence IV states, however, that there is only one railroad track between New London and Hampshire. That is the only section, then, where the two trains could collide. By the time Train B gets to that section, however, Train A will have passed it. The two trains will pass each other somewhere between New London and Kellogsville, not New London and Hampshire.

PREPARING WRITTEN MATERIAL
EXAMINATION SECTION
TEST 1

DIRECTIONS: Each of the sentences in this test may be classified under one of the following four categories:
- A. *Incorrect* because of faulty grammar or sentence structure
- B. *Incorrect* because of faulty punctuation
- C. *Incorrect* because of faulty capitalization
- D. *Correct*

Examine each sentence carefully to determine under which of the above four options it is best classified. Then, in the space at the right, print the capital letter preceding the option which is the BEST of the four suggested above.

(Each incorrect sentence contains but one type of error. Consider a sentence to be correct if it contains none of the types of errors mentioned, even though there may be other correct ways of expressing the same thought.)

1. This fact, together with those brought out at the previous meeting, prove that the schedule is satisfactory to the employees. 1.____

2. Like many employees in scientific fields, the work of bookkeepers and accountants requires accuracy and neatness. 2.____

3. "What can I do for you," the secretary asked as she motioned to the visitor to take a seat. 3.____

4. Our representative, Mr. Charles will call on you next week to determine whether or not your claim has merit. 4.____

5. We expect you to return in the spring; please do not disappoint us. 5.____

6. Any supervisor, who disregards the just complaints of his subordinates, is remiss in the performance of his duty. 6.____

7. Because she took less than an hour for lunch is no reason for permitting her to leave before five o'clock. 7.____

8. "Miss Smith," said the supervisor, "Please arrange a meeting of the staff for two o'clock on Monday." 8.____

9. A private company's vacation and sick leave allowance usually differs considerably from a public agency. 9.____

10. Therefore, in order to increase the efficiency of operations in the department, a report on the recommended changes in procedures was presented to the departmental committee in charge of the program. 10.____

11. We told him to assign the work to whoever was available. 11._____

12. Since John was the most efficient of any other employee in the bureau, he received the highest service rating. 12._____

13. Only those members of the national organization who resided in the middle West attended the conference in Chicago. 13._____

14. The question of whether the office manager has as yet attained, or indeed can ever hope to secure professional status is one which has been discussed for years. 14._____

15. No one knew who to blame for the error which, we later discovered, resulted in a considerable loss of time. 15._____

KEY (CORRECT ANSWERS)

1.	A	6.	B	11.	D
2.	A	7.	A	12.	A
3.	B	8.	C	13.	C
4.	B	9.	A	14.	B
5.	D	10.	D	15.	A

TEST 2

DIRECTIONS: Each of the sentences in this test may be classified under one of the following four categories:
    A. *Incorrect* because of faulty grammar or sentence structure
    B. *Incorrect* because of faulty punctuation
    C. *Incorrect* because of faulty capitalization
    D. *Correct*

1. The National alliance of Businessmen is trying to persuade private businesses to hire youth in the summertime.   1.____

2. The supervisor who is on vacation, is in charge of processing vouchers.   2.____

3. The activity of the committee at its conferences is always stimulating.   3.____

4. After checking the addresses again, the letters went to the mailroom.   4.____

5. The director, as well as the employees, are interested in sharing the dividends.   5.____

KEY (CORRECT ANSWERS)

1. C
2. B
3. D
4. A
5. A

TEST 3

DIRECTIONS: In each of the following groups of sentences, one of the four sentences is faulty in grammar, punctuation, or capitalization. Select the INCORRECT sentence in each case.

1. A. Sailing down the bay was a thrilling experience for me.
   B. He was not consulted about your joining the club.
   C. This story is different than the one I told you yesterday.
   D. There is no doubt about his being the best player.

   1.____

2. A. He maintains there is but one road to world peace.
   B. It is common knowledge that a child sees much he is not supposed to see.
   C. Much of the bitterness might have been avoided if arbitration had been resorted to earlier in the meeting.
   D. The man decided it would be advisable to marry a girl somewhat younger than him.

   2.____

3. A. In this book, the incident I liked least is where the hero tries to put out the forest fire.
   B. Learning a foreign language will undoubtedly give a person a better understanding of his mother tongue.
   C. His actions made us wonder what he planned to do next.
   D. Because of the war, we were unable to travel during the summer vacation.

   3.____

4. A. The class had no sooner become interested in the lesson than the dismissal bell rang.
   B. There is little agreement about the kind of world to be planned at the peace conference.
   C. "Today," said the teacher, "we shall read 'The Wind in the Willows,' I am sure you'll like it.
   D. The terms of the legal settlement of the family quarrel handicapped both sides for many years.

   4.____

5. A. I was so surprised that I was not able to say a word.
   B. She is taller than any other member of the class.
   C. It would be much more preferable if you were never seen in his company.
   D. We had no choice but to excuse her for being late.

   5.____

KEY (CORRECT ANSWERS)

1. C
2. D
3. A
4. C
5. C

TEST 4

DIRECTIONS: In each of the following groups of sentences, one of the four sentences is faulty in grammar, punctuation, or capitalization. Select the INCORRECT sentence in each case.

1. A. Please send me these data at the earliest opportunity.
   B. The loss of their material proved to be a severe handicap.
   C. My principal objection to this plan is that it is impracticable.
   D. The doll had laid in the rain for an hour and was ruined.

   1._____

2. A. The garden scissors, left out all night in the rain, were in a badly rusted condition.
   B. The girls felt bad about the misunderstanding which had arisen
   C. Sitting near the campfire, the old man told John and I about many exciting adventures he had had.
   D. Neither of us is in a position to undertake a task of that magnitude.

   2._____

3. A. The general concluded that one of the three roads would lead to the besieged city.
   B. The children didn't, as a rule, do hardly anything beyond what they were told to do.
   C. The reason the girl gave for her negligence was that she had acted on the spur of the moment.
   D. The daffodils and tulips look beautiful in that blue vase.

   3._____

4. A. If I was ten years older, I should be interested in this work.
   B. Give the prize to whoever has drawn the best picture.
   C. When you have finished reading the book, take it back to the library.
   D. My drawing is as good as or better than yours.

   4._____

5. A. He asked me whether the substance was animal or vegetable.
   B. An apple which is unripe should not be eaten by a child.
   C. That was an insult to me who am your friend.
   D. Some spy must of reported the matter to the enemy.

   5._____

6. A. Limited time makes quoting the entire message impossible.
   B. Who did she say was going?
   C. The girls in your class have dressed more dolls this year than we.
   D. There was such a large amount of books on the floor that I couldn't find a place for my rocking chair.

   6._____

7. A. What with his sleeplessness and his ill health, he was unable to assume any responsibility for the success of the meeting.
   B. If I had been born in February, I should be celebrating my birthday soon.
   C. In order to prevent breakage, she placed a sheet of paper between each of the plates when she packed them.
   D. After the spring shower, the violets smelled very sweet.

   7._____

2 (#4)

8. A. He had laid the book down very reluctantly before the end of the lesson. 8.____
    B. The dog, I am sorry to say, had lain on the bed all night.
    C. The cloth was first lain on a flat surface; then it was pressed with a hot iron.
    D. While we were in Florida, we lay in the sun until we were noticeably tanned.

9. A. If John was in New York during the recent holiday season, I have no doubt 9.____
       he spent most of the time with his parents.
    B. How could he enjoy the television program; the dog was barking and the
       baby was crying.
    C. When the problem was explained to the class, he must have been asleep.
    D. She wished that her new dress were finished so that she could go to the
       party.

10. A. The engine not only furnishes power but light and heat as well. 10.____
    B. You're aware that we've forgotten whose guilt was established, aren't you?
    C. Everybody knows that the woman made many sacrifices for her children.
    D. A man with his dog and gun is a familiar sight in this neighborhood.

KEY (CORRECT ANSWERS)

1.	D	6.	D
2.	C	7.	B
3.	B	8.	C
4.	A	9.	B
5.	D	10.	A

TEST 5

DIRECTIONS: Each of Questions 1 through 5 consists of a sentence which may be classified appropriately under one of the following four categories:
- A. *Incorrect* because of faulty grammar
- B. *Incorrect* because of faulty punctuation
- C. *Incorrect* because of faulty spelling
- D. *Correct*

Examine each sentence carefully. Then, print in the space at the right the letter preceding the category which is the BEST of the four suggested above

(Note: Each incorrect sentence contains only one type of error. Consider a sentence correct if it contains no errors, although there may be other correct ways of writing the sentence.)

1. Of the two employees, the one in our office is the most efficient.   1.____

2. No one can apply or even understand, the new rules and regulations.   2.____

3. A large amount of supplies were stored in the empty office.   3.____

4. If an employee is occassionally asked to work overtime, he should do so willingly.   4.____

5. It is true that the new procedures are difficult to use but, we are certain that you will learn them quickly.   5.____

6. The office manager said that he did not know who would be given a large allotment under the new plan.   6.____

7. It was at the supervisor's request that the clerk agreed to postpone his vacation.   7.____

8. We do not believe that it is necessary for both he and the clerk to attend the conference.   8.____

9. All employees, who display perseverance, will be given adequate recognition.   9.____

10. He regrets that some of us employees are dissatisfied with our new assignments.   10.____

11. "Do you think that the raise was merited," asked the supervisor?   11.____

12. The new manual of procedure is a valuable supplement to our rules and regulations.   12.____

13. The typist admitted that she had attempted to pursuade the other employees to assist her in her work.   13.____

2 (#5)

14. The supervisor asked that all amendments to the regulations be handled by you and I.   14.____

15. The custodian seen the boy who broke the window.   15.____

KEY (CORRECT ANSWERS)

1.	A	6.	D	11.	B
2.	B	7.	D	12.	C
3.	A	8.	A	13.	C
4.	C	9.	B	14.	A
5.	B	10.	D	15.	A

PREPARING WRITTEN MATERIAL

PARAGRAPH REARRANGEMENT
COMMENTARY

The sentences that follow are in scrambled order. You are to rearrange them in proper order and indicate the letter choice containing the correct answer at the space at the right.

Each group of sentences in this section is actually a paragraph presented in scrambled order. Each sentence in the group has a place in that paragraph; no sentence is to be left out. You are to read each group of sentences and decide upon the best order in which to put the sentences so as to form a well-organized paragraph.

The questions in this section measure the ability to solve a problem when all the facts relevant to its solution are not given.

More specifically, certain positions of responsibility and authority require the employee to discover connection between events sometimes, apparently, unrelated. In order to do this, the employee will find it necessary to correctly infer that unspecified events have probably occurred or are likely to occur. This ability becomes especially important when action must be taken on incomplete information.

Accordingly, these questions require competitors to choose among several suggested alternatives, each of which presents a different sequential arrangement of the events. Competitors must choose the MOST logical of the suggested sequences.

In order to do so, they may be required to draw on general knowledge to infer missing concepts or events that are essential to sequencing the given events. Competitors should be careful to infer only what is essential to the sequence. The plausibility of the wrong alternatives will always require the inclusion of unlikely events or of additional chains of events which are NOT essential to sequencing the given events.

It's very important to remember that you are looking for the best of the four possible choices, and that the best choice of all may not even be one of the answers you're given to choose from.

There is no one right way to solve these problems. Many people have found it helpful to first write out the order of the sentences, as they would have arranged them, on their scrap paper before looking at the possible answers. If their optimum answer is there, this can save them some time. If it isn't, this method can still give insight into solving the problem. Others find it most helpful to just go through each of the possible choices, contrasting each as they go along. You should use whatever method feels comfortable and works for you.

While most of these types of questions are not that difficult, we've added a higher percentage of the difficult type, just to give you more practice. Usually there are only one or two questions on this section that contain such subtle distinctions that you're unable to answer confidently. And you then may find yourself stuck deciding between two possible choices, neither of which you're sure about.

EXAMINATION SECTION

TEST 1

DIRECTIONS: The sentences that follow are in scrambled order. You are to rearrange them in proper order and indicate the letter choice containing the correct answer. *PRINT THE LETTER OF THE CORRECT ANSWER IN THE SPACE AT THE RIGHT.*

1. Below are four statements labeled W, X, Y and Z.   1._____
   W. He was a strict and fanatic drillmaster.
   X. The word is always used in a derogatory sense and generally shows resentment and anger on the part of the user.
   Y. It is from the name of this Frenchman that we derive our English word, martinet.
   Z. Jean Martinet was the Inspector-General of Infantry during the reign of King Louis XIV.
   The PROPER order in which these sentences should be placed in a paragraph is:
     A. X, Z, W, Y   B. X, Z, Y, W   C. Z, W, Y, X   D. Z, Y, W, X

2. In the following paragraph, the sentences, which are numbered, have been jumbled.   2._____
   I. Since then it has undergone changes.
   II. It was incorporated in 1955 under the laws of the State of New York.
   III. Its primary purposes, a cleaner city, has, however, remained the same.
   IV. The Citizens Committee works in cooperation with the Mayor's Inter-departmental Committee for a Clean City.   3._____
   The order in which these sentences should be arranged to form a well-organized paragraph is:
     A. II, IV, I, III   B. III, IV, I, II   C. IV, II, I, III   D. IV, III, II, I

Questions 3-5.

DIRECTIONS: The sentences listed below are part of a meaningful paragraph but they are not given in their proper order. You are to decide what would be the BEST order in which to put the sentences so as to form a well-organized paragraph. Each sentence has a place in the paragraph; there are no extra sentences. You are then to answer Questions 3 through 5 inclusive on the basis of your rearrangements of these scrambled sentences into a properly organized paragraph.

In 1887 some insurance companies organized an Inspection Department to advise their clients on all phases of fire prevention and protection. Probably this has been due to the smaller annual fire losses in Great Britain than in the United States. It tests various fire prevention devices and appliances and determines manufacturing hazards and their safeguards. Fire research began earlier in the United States and is more advanced than in Great Britain. Later they established a laboratory specializing in electrical, mechanical, hydraulic, and chemical fields.

123

3. When the five sentences are arranged in proper order, the paragraph starts with the sentence which begins
   A. "In 1887…"
   B. "Probably this…"
   C. "It tests…"
   D. "Fire research…"
   E. "Later they…"

3.____

4. In the last sentence listed above, "they" refers to
   A. the insurance companies
   B. the United States and Great Britain
   C. the Inspection Department
   D. clients
   E. technicians

4.____

5. When the above paragraph is properly arranged, it ends with the words
   A. "…and protection."
   B. "…the United States."
   C. "…their safeguards."
   D. "…in Great Britain."
   E. "…chemical fields."

5.____

KEY (CORRECT ANSWERS)

1. C
2. C
3. D
4. A
5. C

TEST 2

DIRECTIONS: In each of the questions numbered I through V, several sentences are given. For each question, choose as your answer the group of number that represents the MOST logical order of these sentences if they were arranged in paragraph form. *PRINT THE LETTER OF THE CORRECT ANSWER IN THE SPACE AT THE RIGHT.*

1.
   I. It is established when one shows that the landlord has prevented the tenant's enjoyment of his interest in the property leased.
   II. Constructive eviction is the result of a breach of the covenant of quiet enjoyment implied in all leases.
   III. In some parts of the United States, it is not complete until the tenant vacates within a reasonable time.
   IV. Generally, the acts must be of such serious and permanent character as to deny the tenant the enjoyment of his possessing rights.
   V. In this event, upon abandonment of the premises, the tenant's liability for that ceases.
   The CORRECT answer is:
   A. II, I, IV, III, V
   B. V, II, III, I, IV
   C. IV, III, I, II, V
   D. I, III, V, IV, II

   1.____

2.
   I. The powerlessness before private and public authorities that is the typical experience of the slum tenant is reminiscent of the situation of blue-collar workers all through the nineteenth century.
   II. Similarly, in recent years, this chapter of history has been reopened by anti-poverty groups which have attempted to organize slum tenants to enable them to bargain collectively with their landlords about the conditions of their tenancies.
   III. It is familiar history that many of the worker remedied their condition by joining together and presenting their demands collectively.
   IV. Like the workers, tenants are forced by the conditions of modern life into substantial dependence on these who possess great political aid and economic power.
   V. What's more, the very fact of dependence coupled with an absence of education and self-confidence makes them hesitant and unable to stand up for what they need from those in power.
   The CORRECT answer is:
   A. V, IV, I, II, III
   B. II, III, I, V, IV
   C. III, I, V, IV, II
   D. I, IV, V, III, II

   2.____

3.
   I. A railroad, for example, when not acting as a common carrier may contract away responsibility for its own negligence.
   II. As to a landlord, however, no decision has been found relating to the legal effect of a clause shifting the statutory duty of repair to the tenant.
   III. The courts have not passed on the validity of clauses relieving the landlord of this duty and liability.
   IV. They have, however, upheld the validity of exculpatory clauses in other types of contracts.

   3.____

125

V. Housing regulations impose a duty upon the landlord to maintain leased premises in safe condition.
VI. As another example, a bailee may limit his liability except for gross negligence, willful acts, or fraud.

The CORRECT answer is:
A. II, I, VI, IV, III, V
B. I, III, IV, V, VI, II
C. III, V, I, IV, II, VI
D. V, III, IV, I, VI, II

4.
I. Since there are only samples in the building, retail or consumer sales are generally eschewed by mart occupants, and in some instances, rigid controls are maintained to limit entrance to the mart only to those persons engaged in retailing.
II. Since World War I, in many larger cities, there has developed a new type of property, called the mart building.
III. It can, therefore, be used by wholesalers and jobbers for the display of sample merchandise.
IV. This type of building is most frequently a multi-storied, finished interior property which is a cross between a retail arcade and a loft building.
V. This limitation enables the mart occupants to ship the orders from another location after the retailer or dealer makes his selection from the samples.

The CORRECT answer is:
A. II, IV, III, I, V
B. IV, III, V, I, II
C. I, III, II, IV, V
D. I, IV, II, III, V

5.
I. In general, staff-line friction reduces the distinctive contribution of staff personnel.
II. The conflicts, however, introduce an uncontrolled element into the managerial system.
III. On the other hand, the natural resistance of the line to staff innovations probably usefully restrains over-eager efforts to apply untested procedures on a large scale.
IV. Under such conditions, it is difficult to know when valuable ideas are being sacrificed.
V. The relatively weak position of staff, requiring accommodation to the line, tends to restrict their ability to engage in free, experimental innovation.

The CORRECT answer is:
A. IV, II, III, I, V
B. I, V, III, II, IV
C. V, III, I, II, IV
D. II, I, IV, V, III

KEY (CORRECT ANSWERS)

1. A
2. D
3. D
4. A
5. B

TEST 3

DIRECTIONS: Questions 1 through 4 consist of six sentences which can be arranged in a logical sequence. For each question, select the choice which places the numbered sentences in the MOST logical sequent. *PRINT THE LETTER OF THE CORRECT ANSWER IN THE SPACE AT THE RIGHT.*

1.
   I. The burden of proof as to each issue is determined before trial and remains upon the same party throughout the trial.
   II. The jury is at liberty to believe one witness' testimony as against a number of contradictory witnesses.
   III. In a civil case, the party bearing the burden of proof is required to prove his contention by a fair preponderance of the evidence.
   IV. However, it must be noted that a fair preponderance of evidence does not necessarily mean a greater number of witnesses.
   V. The burden of proof is the burden which rests upon one of the parties to an action to persuade the trier of the facts, generally the jury, that a proposition he asserts is true.
   VI. If the evidence is equally balanced, or if it leaves the jury in such doubt as to be unable to decide the controversy either way, judgment must be given against the party upon whom the burden of proof rests.
   The CORRECT answer is:
   A. III, II, V, IV, I, VI
   B. I, II, VI, V, III, IV
   C. III, IV, V, I, II, VI
   D. V, I, III, VI, IV, II

   1.____

2.
   I. If a parent is without assets and is unemployed, he cannot be convicted of the crime of non-support of a child.
   II. The term "sufficient ability" has been held to mean sufficient financial ability.
   III. It does not matter if his unemployment is by choice or unavoidable circumstances.
   IV. If he fails to take any steps at all, he may be liable to prosecution for endangering the welfare of a child.
   V. Under the penal law, a parent is responsible for the support of his minor child only if the parent is "of sufficient ability."
   VI. An indigent parent may meet his obligation by borrowing money or by seeking aid under the provisions of the Social Welfare Law.
   The CORRECT answer is:
   A. VI, I, V, III, II, IV
   B. I, III, V, II, IV, VI
   C. V, II, I, III, VI, IV
   D. I, VI, IV, V, II, III

   2.____

3.
   I. Consider, for example, the case of a rabble rouser who urges a group of twenty people to go out and break the windows of a nearby factory.
   II. Therefore, the law fills the indicated gap with the crime of inciting to riot.
   III. A person is considered guilty of inciting to riot when he urges ten or more persons to engage in tumultuous and violent conduct of a kind likely to create public alarm.
   IV. However, if he has not obtained the cooperation of at least four people, he cannot be charged with unlawful assembly.

   3.____

127

V. The charge of inciting to riot was added to the law to cover types of conduct which cannot be classified as either the crime of "riot" or the crime of "unlawful assembly."
VI. If he acquires the acquiescence of at least four of them, he is guilty of unlawful assembly even if the project does not materialize.

The CORRECT answer is:
A. III, V, I, VI, IV, II
B. V, I, IV, VI, II, III
C. III, IV, I, V, II, VI
D. V, I, IV, VI, III, II

4.
I. If, however, the rebuttal evidence presents an issue of credibility, it is for the jury to determine whether the presumption has, in fact, been destroyed.
II. Once sufficient evidence to the contrary is introduced, the presumption disappears from the trial.
III. The effect of a presumption is to place the burden upon the adversary to come forward with evidence to rebut the presumption.
IV. When a presumption is overcome and ceases to exist in the case, the fact or facts which gave rise to the presumption still remain.
V. Whether a presumption has been overcome is ordinarily a question for the court.
VI. Such information may furnish a basis for a logical inference.

The CORRECT answer is:
A. IV, VI, II, V, I, III
B. III, II, V, I, IV, VI
C. V, III, VI, IV, II, I
D. V, IV, I, II, VI, III

4.____

KEY (CORRECT ANSWERS)

1. D
2. C
3. A
4. B

READING COMPREHENSION
UNDERSTANDING AND INTERPRETING WRITTEN MATERIAL
EXAMINATION SECTION
TEST 1

DIRECTIONS: Each question or incomplete statement is followed by several suggested answers or completions. Select the one that BEST answers the question or completes the statement. *PRINT THE LETTER OF THE CORRECT ANSWER IN THE SPACE AT THE RIGHT.*

Questions 1-5.

DIRECTIONS: Questions 1 through 5 are to be answered SOLELY on the basis of the following passage.

The most effective control mechanism to prevent gross incompetence on the part of public employees is a good personnel program. The personnel officer in the line departments and the central personnel agency should exert positive leadership to raise levels of performance. Although the key factor is the quality of the personnel recruited, staff members other than personnel officers can make important contributions to efficiency. Administrative analysts, now employed in many agencies, make detailed studies of organization and procedures, with the purpose of eliminating delays, waste, and other inefficiencies. Efficiency is, however, more than a question of good organization and procedures; it is also the product of the attitudes and value of the public employees. Personal motivation can provide the will to be efficient. The best management studies will not result in substantial improvement of the performance of those employees who feel no great urge to wok up to their abilities.

1. The above passage indicates that the KEY factor in preventing gross incompetence of public employees is the
   A. hiring of administrative analysts to assist personnel people
   B. utilization of effective management studies
   C. overlapping of responsibility
   D. quality of the employees hired

   1.____

2. According to the above passage, the central personnel agency staff SHOULD
   A. work more closely with administrative analysts in the line departments than with personnel officers
   B. make a serious effort to avoid jurisdictional conflicts with personnel officers in line departments
   C. contribute to improving the quality of work of public employees
   D. engage in a comprehensive program to change the public's negative image of public employees

   2.____

3. The above passage indicates that efficiency in an organization can BEST be   3._____
   brought about by
   A. eliminating ineffective control mechanisms
   B. instituting sound organizational procedures
   C. promoting competent personnel
   D. recruiting people with desire to do good work

4. According to the above passage, the purpose of administrative analysts   4._____
   in a public agency is to
   A. prevent injustice to the public employee
   B. promote the efficiency of the agency
   C. protect the interests of the public
   D. ensure the observance of procedural due process

5. The above passage implies that a considerable rise in the quality of work of   5._____
   public employees can be brought about by
   A. encouraging positive employee attitudes toward work
   B. controlling personnel officers who exceed their powers
   C. creating warm personal associations among public employees in an agency
   D. closing loopholes in personnel organization and procedures

Questions 6-8.

DIRECTIONS: Questions 6 through 8 are to be answered SOLELY on the basis of the following passage.

EMPLOYEE NEEDS

The greatest waste in industry and in government may be that of human resources. This waste usually derives not from employees' unwillingness or inability, but from management's ineptness to meet the maintenance and motivational needs of employees. Maintenance needs refer to such needs as providing employees with safe places to work, written work rules, job security, adequate salary, employer-sponsored social activities, and with knowledge of their role in the overall framework of the organization. However, of greatest significance to employees are the motivational needs of job growth, achievement, responsibility, and recognition.

Although employee dissatisfaction may stem from either poor maintenance or poor motivation factors, the outward manifestation of the dissatisfaction may be very much like, i.e., negativism, complaints, deterioration of performance, and so forth. The improvement in the lighting of an employee's work area or raising his level of ay won't do much good if the source of the dissatisfaction is the absence of a meaningful assignment. By the same token, if an employee is dissatisfied with what he considers inequitable pay, the introduction of additional challenge in his work may simply make matters worse.

It is relatively easy for an employee to express frustration by complaining about pay, washroom conditions, fringe benefits, and so forth; but most people cannot easily express resentment in terms of the more abstract concepts concerning job growth, responsibility, and achievement.

It would be wrong to assume that there is no interaction between maintenance and motivational needs of employee. For example, conditions of high motivation often overshadow poor maintenance conditions. If an organization is in a period of strong growth and expansion, opportunities for job growth, responsibility, recognition, and achievement are usually abundant, but the rapid growth may have outrun the upkeep of maintenance factors. In this situation, motivation may be high, but only if employees recognize the poor maintenance conditions as unavoidable and temporary. The subordination of maintenance factors cannot go on indefinitely, even with the highest motivation.

Both maintenance and motivation factors influence the behavior of all employees, but employees are not identical and, furthermore, the needs of any individual do not remain orientation toward maintenance factors and those with greater sensitivity toward motivation factors.

A highly maintenance-oriented individual, preoccupied with the factors peripheral to his job rather than the job itself, is more concerned with comfort than challenge. He does not get deeply involved with his work but does with the condition of his work area, toilet facilities, and his time for going to lunch. By contrast, a strongly motivation-oriented employee is usually relatively indifferent to his surroundings and is caught up in the pursuit of work goals.

Fortunately, there are few people who are either exclusively maintenance-oriented or purely motivation-oriented. The former would be deadwood in an organization, while the latter might trample on those around him in his pursuit to achieve his goals.

6. With respect to employee motivational and maintenance needs, the management policies of an organization which is growing rapidly will probably result
    A. more in meeting motivational needs rather than maintenance needs
    B. more in meeting maintenance needs rather than motivational needs
    C. in meeting both of these needs equally
    D. in increased effort to define the motivational and maintenance needs of its employees

7. In accordance with the above passage, which of the following CANNOT be considered as an example of an employee maintenance need for railroad clerks?
    A. Providing more relief periods
    B. Providing fair salary increases at periodic intervals
    C. Increasing job responsibilities
    D. Increasing health insurance benefits

8. Most employees in an organization may be categorized as being interested in
    A. maintenance needs only
    B. motivational needs only
    C. both motivational and maintenance needs
    D. money only, to the exclusion of all other needs

Questions 9-11.

DIRECTIONS: Questions 9 through 11 are to be answered SOLELY on the basis of the following passage.

GOOD EMPLOYEE PRACTICES

As a city employee, you will be expected to take an interest in you work and perform the duties of your job to the best of your ability and in a spirit of cooperation. Nothing shows an interest in your work more than coming to work on time, not only at the start of the day but also when returning from lunch. If it is necessary for you to keep a personal appointment at lunch hour which might cause a delay in getting back to work on time, you should explain the situation to your supervisor and get his approval to come back a little late before you leave for lunch.

You should do everything that is asked of you willingly and consider important even the small jobs that your supervisor gives you. Although these jobs may seem unimportant, if you forget to do them or if you don't do them right, trouble may develop later.

Getting along well with your fellow workers will add much to the enjoyment of your work. You should respect your fellow workers and try to see their side when a disagreement arises. The better you get along with your fellow workers and your supervisor, the better you will like your job and the better you will be able to do it.

9. According to the above passage, in your job as a city employee, you are expected to
   A. show a willingness to cooperate on the job
   B. get your supervisor's approval before keeping any personal appointments at lunch hour
   C. avoid doing small jobs that seem unimportant
   D. do the easier jobs at the start of the day and the more difficult ones later on

9._____

10. According to the above passage, getting to work on time shows that you
    A. need the job
    B. have an interest in your work
    C. get along well with your fellow workers
    D. like your supervisor

10._____

11. According to the above passage, the one of the following statements that is NOT true is:
    A. If you do a small job wrong, trouble may develop
    B. You should respect your fellow workers
    C. If you disagree with a fellow worker, you should try to see his side of the story
    D. The less you get along with your supervisor, the better you will be able to do your job

11._____

Questions 12-15.

DIRECTIONS: Questions 12 through 15 are to be answered SOLELY on the basis of the following passage.

EMPLOYEE SUGGESTIONS

To increase the effectiveness of the city government, the city asks its employees to offer suggestions when they feel an improvement could be made in some government operation. The Employees' Suggestions Program was started to encourage city employees to do this. Through this Program, which is only for city employees, cash awards may be given to those whose suggestions are submitted and approved. Suggestions are looked for not only from supervisors but from all city employees as any city employee may get an idea which might be approved and contribute greatly to the solution of some problem of city government.

Therefore, all suggestions for improvement are welcome, whether they be suggestions on how to improve working conditions, or on how to increase the speed with which work is done, or on how to reduce or eliminate such things as waste, time losses, accidents or fire hazards. There are, however, a few types of suggestions for which cash awards cannot be given. An example of this type would be a suggestion to increase salaries or a suggestion to change the regulations about annual leave or about sick leave. The number of suggestions sent in has increased sharply during the past few years. It is hoped that it will keep increasing in the future in order to meet the city's needs for more ideas for improved ways of doing things.

12. According to the above passage, the MAIN reason why the city asks its employees for suggestions about government operations is to
    A. increase the effectiveness of the city government
    B. show that the Employees' Suggestion Program is working well
    C. show that everybody helps run the city government
    D. have the employee win a prize

13. According to the above passage, the Employees' Suggestion Program can approve awards ONLY for those suggestions that come from
    A. city employees
    B. city employees who are supervisors
    C. city employees who are not supervisors
    D. experienced employee of the city

14. According to the above passage, a cash award cannot be given through the Employees' Suggestion Program for a suggestion about
    A. getting work done faster
    B. helping prevent accidents on the job
    C. increasing the amount of annual leave for city employees
    D. reducing the chance of fire where city employees work

15. According to the above passage, the suggestions sent in during the past few years have 15.____
    A. all been approved
    B. generally been well written
    C. been mostly about reducing or eliminating waste
    D. been greater in number than before

Questions 16-18.

DIRECTIONS: Questions 16 through 18 are to be answered SOLELY on the basis of the following passage.

    The supervisor will gain the respect of the members of his staff and increase his influence over them by controlling his temper and avoiding criticizing anyone publicly. When a mistake is made, the good supervisor will take it over with the employee quietly and privately. The supervisor will listen to the employee's story, suggest the better way of doing the job, and offer help so the mistake won't happen again. Before closing the discussion, the supervisor should try to find something good to say about other parts of the employee's work. Some praise and appreciation, along with instruction, is more likely to encourage an employee to improve in those areas where he is weakest.

16. A good title that would show the meaning of the above passage would be 16.____
    A. How to Correct Employee Errors
    B. How to Praise Employees
    C. Mistakes are Preventable
    D. The Weak Employee

17. According to the above passage, the work of an employee who has made a mistake is more likely to improve if the supervisor 17.____
    A. avoids criticizing him
    B. gives him a chance to suggest a better way of doing the work
    C. listens to the employee's excuses to see if he is right
    D. praises good work at the same time he corrects the mistake

18. According to the above passage, when a supervisor needs to correct an employee's mistake, it is important that he 18.____
    A. allow some time to go by after the mistake is made
    B. do so when other employee are not present
    C. show his influence with his tone of voice
    D. tell other employee to avoid the same mistake

Questions 19-23.

DIRECTIONS: Questions 19 through 23 are to be answered SOLELY on the basis of the following passage.

    In studying the relationships of people to the organizational structure, it is absolutely necessary to identify and recognize the informal organizational structure. These relationships are necessary when coordination of a plan is attempted. They may be with *the boss*, line supervisors, staff personnel, or other representatives of the formal organization's hierarchy, and they may include the *liaison men* who serve as the leaders of the informal organization. An acquaintanceship with the people serving in these roles in the organization, and its formal counterpart, permits a supervisor to recognize sensitive areas in which it is simple to get conflict reaction. Avoidance of such areas, plus conscious efforts to inform other people of his own objectives for various plans, will usually enlist their aid and support. Planning *without* people can lead to disaster because the individuals who must act together to make any plan a success are more important than the plans themselves.

19. Of the following titles, the one that MOST clearly describes the above passage is
    A. Coordination of a Function
    B. Avoidance of Conflict
    C. Planning With People
    D. Planning Objectives

20. According to the above passage, attempts at coordinating plans may fail unless
    A. the plan's objectives are clearly set forth
    B. conflict between groups is resolved
    C. the plans themselves are worthwhile
    D. informal relationships are recognized

21. According to the above passage, conflict
    A. may, in some cases, be desirable to secure results
    B. produces more heat than light
    C. should be avoided at all costs
    D. possibilities can be predicted by a sensitive supervisor

22. The above passage implies that
    A. informal relationships are more important than formal structure
    B. the weakness of a formal structure depends upon informal relationships
    C. liaison men are the key people to consult when taking formal and informal structures into account
    D. individuals in a group are at least as important as the plans for the group

23. The above passage suggests that
    A. some planning can be disastrous
    B. certain people in sensitive areas should be avoided
    C. the supervisor should discourage acquaintanceships in the organization
    D. organizational relationships should be consciously limited

Questions 24-25.

DIRECTIONS: Questions 24 and 25 are to be answered SOLELY on the basis of the following passage.

Good personnel relations of an organization depend upon mutual confidence, trust, and good will. The basis of confidence is understanding. Most troubles start with people who do not understand each other. When the organization's intentions or motives are misunderstood, or when reasons for actions, practices, or policies are misconstrued, complete cooperation from individuals is not forthcoming. If management expects full cooperation from employees, it has a responsibility of sharing with them the information which is the foundation of proper understanding, confidence, and trust. Personnel management has long since outgrown the days when it was the vogue to *treat them rough and tell them nothing*. Up-to-date personnel management provides all possible information about the activities, aims, and purposes of the organization. It seems altogether creditable that a desire should exist among employees for such information which the best-intentioned executive might think would not interest them and which the worst-intentioned would think was none of their business.

24. The above passage implies that one of the causes of the difficulty which an organization might have with its personnel relations is that its employees
    A. have not expressed interest in the activities, aims, and purposes of the organization
    B. do not believe in the good faith of the organization
    C. have not been able to give full cooperation to the organization
    D. do not recommend improvements in the practices and policies of the organization

24.____

25. According to the above passage, in order for an organization to have good personnel relations, it is NOT essential that
    A. employees have confidence in the organization
    B. the purposes of the organization be understood by the employees
    C. employees have a desire for information about the organization
    D. information about the organization be communicated to employees

25.____

KEY (CORRECT ANSWERS)

1.	D	11.	D
2.	C	12.	A
3.	D	13.	A
4.	B	14.	C
5.	A	15.	D
6.	A	16.	A
7.	C	17.	D
8.	C	18.	B
9.	A	19.	C
10.	B	20.	D

21. D
22. D
23. A
24. B
25. C

TEST 2

DIRECTIONS: Each question or incomplete statement is followed by several suggested answers or completions. Select the one that BEST answers the question or completes the statement. *PRINT THE LETTER OF THE CORRECT ANSWER IN THE SPACE AT THE RIGHT.*

Questions 1-8.

DIRECTIONS: Questions 1 through 8 are to be answered SOLELY on the basis of the following passage.

Important figures in education and in public affairs have recommended development of a private organization sponsored in part by various private foundations which would offer installment payment plans to full-time matriculated students in accredited colleges and universities in the United States and Canada. Contracts would be drawn to cover either tuition and fees, or tuition, fees, room and board in college facilities, from one year up to and including six years. A special charge, which would vary with the length of the contract, would be added to the gross repayable amount. This would be in addition to interest at a rate which would vary with the income of the parents. There would be a 3% annual interest charge for families with total income, before income taxes, of $50,000 or less. The rate would increase by 1/10 of 1% for every $1,000 of additional net income in excess of $50,000 up to a maximum of 10% interest. Contracts would carry an insurance provision on the life of the parent or guardian who signs the contract; all contracts must have the signature of a parent or guardian. Payment would be scheduled in equal monthly installments.

1. Which of the following students would be eligible for the payment plan described in the above passage? A
    A. matriculated student taking six semester hours toward a graduate degree
    B. matriculated student taking seventeen semester hours toward an undergraduate degree
    C. graduate matriculated at the University of Mexico taking eighteen semester hours toward a graduate degree
    D. student taking eighteen semester hours in a special pre-matriculation program

1._____

2. According to the above passage, the organization described would be sponsored in part by
    A. private foundations   B. colleges and universities
    C. persons in the field of education   D. persons in public life

2._____

3. Which of the following expenses could NOT be covered by a contract with the organization described in the above passage?
    A. Tuition amounting to $20,000 per year
    B. Registration and laboratory fees
    C. Meals at restaurants near the college
    D. Rent for an apartment in a college dormitory

3._____

4. The total amount to be paid would include ONLY the
   A. principal
   B. principal and interest
   C. principal, interest, and special charge
   D. principal, interest, special charge, and fee

5. The contract would carry insurance on the
   A. life of the student
   B. life of the student's parents
   C. income of the parents of the student
   D. life of the parent who signed the contract

6. The interest rate for an annual loan of $25,000 from the organization described in the above passage for a student whose family's net income was $55,000 should be
   A. 3%   B. 3.5%   C. 4%   D. 4.5%

7. The interest rate for an annual loan of $35,000 from the organization described in the above passage for a student whose family's net income was $100,000 should be
   A. 5%   B. 8%   C. 9%   D. 10%

8. John Lee has submitted an application for the installment payment plan described in the above passage. John's mother and father have a store which grossed $500,000 last year, but the income which the family received from the store was $90,000 before taxes. They also had $5,000 income from stock dividends. They paid $10,000 in income taxes.
   The amount of income upon which the interest should be based is
   A. $85,000   B. $90,000   C. $95,000   D. $105,000

Questions 9-13.

DIRECTIONS: Questions 9 through 13 are to be answered SOLELY on the basis of the following passage.

Since the organization chart is pictorial in nature, there is a tendency for it to be drawn in an artistically balanced and appealing fashion, regardless of the realities of actual organizational structure. In addition to being subject to this distortion, there is the difficulty of communicating in any organization chart the relative importance or the relative size of various component parts of an organizational structure. Furthermore, because of the need for simplicity of design, an organization chart can never indicate the full extent of the interrelationships among the component parts of an organization.

These interrelationships are often just as vital as the specifications which an organization chart endeavors to indicate. Yet, if an organization chart were to be drawn with all the wide variety of criss-crossing communication and cooperation networks existent within a typical organization, the chart would probably be much more confusing than informative. It is also obvious that no organization chart as such can prove or disprove that the organizational structure it represents is effective in realizing the objectives of the organization. At best, an organization chart can only illustrate some of the various factors to be taken into consideration in understanding, devising, or altering organizational arrangements.

9. According to the above passage, an organization chart can be expected to portray the
    A. structure of the organization along somewhat ideal lines
    B. relative size of the organizational units quite accurately
    C. channels of information distribution within the organization graphically
    D. extent of the obligation of each unit to meet the organizational objectives

9.____

10. According to the above passage, those aspects of internal functioning which are NOT shown on an organization chart
    A. can be considered to have little practical application in the operations of the organization
    B. might well be considered to be as important as the structural relationships which a chart does present
    C. could be the cause of considerable confusion in the operations of an organization which is quite large
    D. would be most likely to provide the information needed to determine the overall effectiveness of an organization

10.____

11. In the above passage, the one of the following conditions which is NOT implied as being a defect of an organization chart is that an organization chart may
    A. present a picture of the organizational structure which is different from the structure that actually exists
    B. fail to indicate the comparative size of various organizational units
    C. be limited in its ability to convey some of the meaningful aspects of organizational relationships
    D. become less useful over a period of time during which the organizational facts which it illustrated have changed

11.____

12. The one of the following which is the MOST suitable title for the above passage is
    A. The Design and Construction of an Organization Chart
    B. The Informal Aspects of an Organization Chart
    C. The Inherent Deficiencies of an Organization Chart
    D. The Utilization of a Typical Organization Chart

12.____

13. It can be inferred from the above passage that the function of an organization chart is to
    A. contribute to the comprehension of the organization form and arrangements
    B. establish the capabilities of the organization to operate effectively
    C. provide a balanced picture of the operations of the organization
    D. eliminate the need for complexity in the organization's structure

13.____

Questions 14-16.

DIRECTIONS: Questions 14 through 16 are to be answered SOLELY on the basis of the following passage.

In dealing with visitors to the school office, the school secretary must use initiative, tact, and good judgment. All visitors should be greeted promptly and courteously. The nature of their business should be determined quickly and handled expeditiously. Frequently, the secretary should be able to handle requests, deliveries, or passes herself. Her judgment should determine when a visitor should see members of the staff or the principal. Serious problems or doubtful cases should be referred to a supervisor.

14. In general, visitors should be handled by the 14.____
 A. school secretary B. principal
 C. appropriate supervisor D. person who is free

15. It is wise to obtain the following information from visitors: 15.____
 A. Name B. Nature of business
 C. Address D. Problems they have

16. All visitors who wish to see members of the staff should 16.____
 A. be permitted to do so B. produce identification
 C. do so for valid reasons only D. be processed by a supervisor

Questions 17-19.

DIRECTIONS: Questions 17 through 19 are to be answered SOLELY on the basis of the following passage.

Information regarding payroll status, salary differentials, promotional salary increments, deductions, and pension payments should be given to all members of the staff who have questions regarding these items. On occasion, if the secretary is uncertain regarding the information, the staff member should be referred to the principal or the appropriate agency. No question by a staff member regarding payroll status should be brushed aside as immaterial or irrelevant. The school secretary must always try to handle the question or pass it on to the person who can handle it.

17. If a teacher is dissatisfied with information regarding her salary status, as given 17.____
 by the school secretary, the matter should be
 A. dropped
 B. passed on to the principal
 C. passed on by the secretary to proper agency or the principal
 D. made a basis for grievance procedures

18. The following is an adequate summary of the above passage: 18.____
 A. The secretary must handle all payroll matters
 B. The secretary must handle all payroll matter or know who can handle them
 C. The secretary or the principal must handle all payroll matters
 D. Payroll matter too difficult to handle must be followed up until they are solved

19. The above passage implies that
    A. many teachers ask immaterial questions regarding payroll status
    B. few teachers ask irrelevant pension questions
    C. no teachers ask immaterial salary questions
    D. no question regarding salary should be considered irrelevant

Questions 20-22.

DIRECTIONS: Questions 20 through 22 are to be answered SOLELY on the basis of the following passage.

The necessity for good speech on the part of the school secretary cannot be overstated. The school secretary must deal with the general public, the pupils, the members of the staff, and the school supervisors. In every situation which involves the general public, the secretary serves as a representative of the school. In dealing with pupils, the secretary's speech must serve as a model from which students may guide themselves. Slang, colloquialisms, malapropisms, and local dialects must be avoided.

20. The above passage implies that the speech pattern of the secretary must be
    A. perfect
    B. very good
    C. average
    D. on a level with that of the pupils

21. The last sentence indicates that slang
    A. is acceptable
    B. occurs in all speech
    C. might be used occasionally
    D. should be shunned

22. The above passage implies that the speech of pupils
    A. may be influenced
    B. does not change readily
    C. is generally good
    D. is generally poor

Questions 23-25.

DIRECTIONS: Questions 23 through 25 are to be answered SOLELY on the basis of the following passage.

The school secretary who is engaged in the task of filing records and correspondence should follow a general set of rules. Items which are filed should be available to other secretaries or to supervisors quickly and easily by means of the application of a modicum of common sense and good judgment. Items which, by their nature, may be difficult to find should be cross-indexed. Folders and drawers should be neatly and accurately labeled. There should never be a large accumulation of papers which have not been filed.

23. A good general rule to follow in filing is that materials should be
    A. placed in folders quickly
    B. neatly stored
    C. readily available
    D. cross-indexed

24. Items that are filed should be available to
    A. the secretary charged with the task of filing
    B. secretaries and supervisors
    C. school personnel
    D. the principal

25. A modicum of common sense means _____ common sense.
    A. an average amount of   B. a great deal of
    C. a little   D. no

KEY (CORRECT ANSWERS)

1. B
2. A
3. C
4. C
5. D

6. B
7. B
8. C
9. A
10. B

11. D
12. C
13. A
14. A
15. B

16. C
17. C
18. B
19. D
20. B

21. D
22. A
23. C
24. B
25. C

TEST 3

DIRECTIONS: Each question or incomplete statement is followed by several suggested answers or completions. Select the one that BEST answers the question or completes the statement. *PRINT THE LETTER OF THE CORRECT ANSWER IN THE SPACE AT THE RIGHT.*

Questions 1-4.

DIRECTIONS: Questions 1 through 4 are to be answered SOLELY on the basis of the following passage.

The proposition that administrative activity is essentially the same in all organizations appears to underlie some of the practices in the administration of private higher education. Although the practice is unusual in public education, there are numerous instances of industrial, governmental, or military administrators being assigned to private institutions of higher education and, to a lesser extent, of college and university presidents assuming administrative positions in other types of organizations. To test this theory that administrators are interchangeable, there is a need for systematic observation and classification. The myth that an educational administrator must first have experience in the teaching profession is firmly rooted in a long tradition that has historical prestige. The myth is bound up in the expectations of the public and personnel surrounding the administrator. Since administrative success depends significantly on how well an administrator meets the expectations others have of him, the myth may be more powerful than the special experience in helping the administrator attain organizational and educational objectives. Educational administrators who have risen through the teaching profession have often expressed nostalgia for the life of a teacher or scholar, but there is no evidence that this nostalgia contributes to administrative success.

1. Which of the following statements as completed is MOST consistent with the above passage?
   The greatest number of administrators has moved from
   A. industry and the military to government and universities
   B. government and universities to industry and the military
   C. government, the armed forces, and industry to colleges and universities
   D. colleges and universities to government, the armed forces, and industry

   1._____

2. Of the following, the MOST reasonable inference from the above passage is that a specific area requiring further research is the
   A. place of myth in the tradition and history of the educational profession
   B. relative effectiveness of educational administrators from inside and outside the teaching profession
   C. performance of administrators in the administration of public colleges
   D. degree of reality behind the nostalgia for scholarly pursuits often expressed by educational administrators

   2._____

3. According to the above passage, the value to an educational administrator of experience in the teaching profession
   A. lies in the first-hand knowledge he has acquired of immediate educational problems
   B. may lie in the belief of his colleagues, subordinates, and the public that such experience is necessary
   C. has been supported by evidence that the experience contributes to administrative success in educational fields
   D. would be greater if the administrator were able to free himself from nostalgia for his former duties

4. Of the following, the MOST suitable title for the above passage is
   A. Educational Administration, Its Problems
   B. The Experience Needed For Educational Administration
   C. Administration in Higher Education
   D. Evaluating Administrative Experience

Questions 5-6.

DIRECTIONS: Questions 5 and 6 are to be answered SOLELY on the basis of the following passage.

Management by objectives (MBO) may be defined as the process by which the superior and the subordinate managers of an organization jointly define its common goals, define each individual's major areas of responsibility in terms of the results expected of him and use these measure as guides for operating the unit and assessing the contribution of each of its members.

The MBO approach requires that after organizational goals are established and communicated, targets must be set for each individual position which are congruent with organizational goals. Periodic performance reviews and a final review using the objectives set as criteria are also basic to this approach.

Recent studies have shown that MBO programs are influenced by attitudes and perceptions of the boss, the company, the reward-punishment system, and the program itself. In addition, the manner in which the MBO program is carried out can influence the success of the program. A study done in the late sixties indicates that the best results are obtained when the manager sets goals which deal with significant problem areas in the organizational unit, or with the subordinate's personal deficiencies. These goals must be clear with regard to what is expected of the subordinate. The frequency of feedback is also important in the success of a management-by-objectives program. Generally, the greater the amount of feedback, the more successful the MBO program.

5. According to the above passage, the expected output for individual employees should be determined
   A. after a number of reviews of work performance
   B. after common organizational goals are defined
   C. before common organizational goals are defined
   D. on the basis of an employee's personal qualities

6. According to the above passage, the management-by-objectives approach requires
    A. less feedback than other types of management programs
    B. little review of on-the-job performance after the initial setting of goals
    C. general conformance between individual goals and organizational goals
    D. the setting of goals which deal with minor problem areas in the organization

Questions 7-10.

DIRECTIONS: Questions 7 through 10 are to be answered SOLELY on the basis of the following passage.

   Management, which is the function of executive leadership, has as its principal phases the planning, organizing, and controlling of the activities of subordinate groups in the accomplishment of organizational objectives. Planning specifies the kind and extent of the factors, forces, and effects, and the relationships among them, that will be required for satisfactory accomplishment. The nature of the objectives and their requirements must be known before determinations can be made as to what must be done, how it must be done and why, where actions should take place, who should be responsible, and similar programs pertaining to the formulation of a plan. Organizing, which creates the conditions that must be present before the execution of the plan can be undertaken successfully, cannot be done intelligently without knowledge of the organizational objectives. Control, which has to do with the constraint and regulation of activities entering into the execution of the plan, must be exercised in accordance with the characteristics and requirements of the activities demanded by the plan.

7. The one of the following which is the MOST suitable title for the above passage is
    A. The Nature of Successful Organization
    B. The Planning of Management Functions
    C. The Importance of Organizational Functions
    D. The Principle Aspects of Management

8. It can be inferred from the above passage that the one of the following functions whose existence is essential to the existence of the other three is the
    A. regulation of the work needed to carry out a plan
    B. understanding of what the organization intends to accomplish
    C. securing of information of the factors necessary for accomplishment of objectives
    D. establishment of the conditions required for successful action

9. The one of the following which would NOT be included within any of the principal phases of the function of executive leadership as defined in the above passage is
    A. determination of manpower requirements
    B. procurement of required material
    C. establishment of organizational objectives
    D. scheduling of production

10. The conclusion which can MOST reasonably be drawn from the above passage is that the control phase of managing is most directly concerned with the
    A. influencing of policy determinations
    B. administering of suggestion systems
    C. acquisition of staff for the organization
    D. implementation of performance standards

10.____

Questions 11-12.

DIRECTIONS: Questions 11 and 12 are to be answered SOLELY on the basis of the following passage.

Under an open-and-above-board policy, it is to be expected that some supervisors will gloss over known shortcomings of subordinates rather than face the task of discussing team face-to-face. It is also to be expected that at least some employees whose job performance is below par will reject the supervisor's appraisal as biased and unfair. Be that as it may, these are inescapable aspects of any performance appraisal system in which human beings are involved. The supervisor who shies away from calling a spade a spade, as well as the employee with a chip on his shoulder, will each in his own way eventually be revealed in his true light—to the benefit of the organization as a whole.

11. The BEST of the following interpretations of the above passage is that
    A. the method of rating employee performance requires immediate revision to improve employee acceptance
    B. substandard performance ratings should be discussed with employees even if satisfactory ratings are not
    C. supervisors run the risk of being called unfair by the subordinates even though their appraisals are accurate
    D. any system of employee performance rating is satisfactory if used properly

11.____

12. The BEST of the following interpretations of the above passage is that
    A. supervisors generally are not open-and-above-board with their subordinates
    B. it is necessary for supervisors to tell employees objectively how they are performing
    C. employees complain when their supervisor does not keep them informed
    D. supervisors are afraid to tell subordinates their weaknesses

12.____

Questions 13-15.

DIRECTIONS: Questions 13 through 15 are to be answered SOLELY on the basis of the following passage.

During the last decade, a great deal of interest has been generated around the phenomenon of *organizational development,* or the process of developing human resources through conscious organization effort. Organizational development (OD) stresses improving interpersonal relationships and organizational skills, such as communication, to a much greater degree than individual training ever did. The kind of training that an organization should emphasize depends upon the present and future structure of the organization. If future organizations are to be unstable, shifting coalitions, then individual skills and abilities, particularly those emphasizing innovativeness, creativity, flexibility, and the latest technological knowledge, are crucial and individual training is most appropriate.

But if there is to be little change in organizational structure, then the main thrust of training should be group-oriented or organizational development. This approach seems better designed for overcoming hierarchical barriers, for developing a degree of interpersonal relationships which make communication along the chain of command possible, and for retaining a modicum of innovation and/or flexibility.

13. According to the above passage, group-oriented training is MOST useful in in
    A. developing a communications system that will facilitate understanding through the chain of command
    B. highly flexible and mobile organizations
    C. preventing the crossing of hierarchical barriers within an organization
    D. saving energy otherwise wasted on developing methods of dealing with rigid hierarchies

14. The one of the following conclusions which can be drawn MOST appropriately from the above passage is that
    A. behavioral research supports the use of organizational development training methods rather than individualized training
    B. it is easier to provide individualized training in specific skills than to set up sensitivity training programs
    C. organizational development eliminates innovative or flexible activity
    D. the nature of an organization greatly influences which training methods will be most effective

15. According to the above passage, the one of the following which is LEAST important for large-scale organizations geared to rapid and abrupt change is
    A. current technological information
    B. development of a high degree of interpersonal relationships
    C. development of individual skills and abilities
    D. emphasis on creativity

Questions 16-18.

DIRECTIONS: Questions 16 through 18 are to be answered SOLELY on the basis of the following passage.

The increase in the extent to which each individual is personally responsible to others is most noticeable in a large bureaucracy. No one person *decides* anything; each decision of any importance, is the product of an intricate process of brokerage involving individuals inside and outside the organization who feel some reason to be affected by the decision, or two have special knowledge to contribute to it. The more varied the organization's constituency, the more inside *veto-groups* will need to be taken into account. But even if no outside consultations were involved, sheer size would produce a complex process of decision. For a large organization is a deliberately created system of tensions into which each individual is expected to bring work-ways, viewpoints, and outside relationships markedly different from those of his colleagues. It is the administrator's task to draw from these disparate forces the elements of wise action from day to day, consistent with the purposes of the organization as a whole.

16. The above passage is essentially a description of decision-making as 16.____
    A. an organization process
    B. the key responsibility of the administrator
    C. the one best position among many
    D. a complex of individual decisions

17. Which one of the following statements BEST describes the responsibilities of 17.____
    an administrator?
    A. He modifies decisions and goals in accordance with pressures from within and outside the organization.
    B. He creates problem-solving mechanisms that rely on the varied interests of his staff and *veto-groups*.
    C. He makes determinations that will lead to attainment of his agency's objectives.
    D. He obtains agreement among varying viewpoints and interests

18. In the context of the operations of a central public personnel agency, a 18.____
    veto-group would LEAST likely consist of
    A. employee organizations
    B. professional personnel societies
    C. using agencies
    D. civil service newspapers

Questions 19-25.

DIRECTIONS: Questions 19 through 25 are to be answered SOLELY on the basis of the following passage, which is an extract from a report prepared for Department X, which outlines the procedure to be followed in the case of transfers of employees.

Every transfer, regardless of the reason therefore, requires completion of the record of transfer, Form DT411. To denote consent to the transfer, DT411 should contain the signatures of the transferee and the personnel officer(s) concerned, except that, in the case of an involuntary transfer, the signatures of the transferee's present and prospective supervisors shall be entered in Boxes 8A and 8B, respectively, since the transferee does not consent. Only a permanent employee may request a transfer; in such cases, the employee's attendance record shall be duly considered with regard to absences, latenesses, and accrued overtime balances. In the case of an inter-district transfer, the employee's attendance record must be included in Section 8A of the transfer request, Form DT410, by the personnel officer of the district from which the transfer is requested. The personnel officer of the district to which the employee requested transfer may refuse to accept accrued overtime balances in excess of ten days.

An employee on probation shall be eligible for transfer. If such employee is involuntarily transferred, he shall be credited for the period of time already served on probation. However, if such transfer is voluntary, the employee shall be required to serve the entire period of his probation in the new position. An employee who has occurred a disability which prevents him from performing his normal duties may be transferred during the period of such disability to other appropriate duties. A disability transfer requires the completion of either DT414 if the disability is job-connected, or Form DT415 if it is not a job-connected disability. In either case, the personnel officer of the district from which the transfer is made signs in Box 6A of the first two copies and the personnel officer of the district to which the transfer is made signs in Box 6B of the last two copies, or, in the case of an intra-district disability transfer, the personnel officer must sign in Box 6A of the first two copies and Box 6B of the last two copies.

19. When a personnel officer consents to an employee's request for transfer from his district, this procedure requires that the personnel officer sign Forms
    A. DT411
    B. DT410 and DT411
    C. DT411 and either Form DT414 or DT415
    D. DT410 and DT411, and either Form DT414 or DT415

20. With respect to the time record of an employee transferred against his wishes during his probationary period, this procedure requires that
    A. he serve the entire period of his probation in his present office
    B. he lose his accrued overtime balance
    C. his attendance record be considered with regard to absences and latenesses
    D. he be given credit for the period of time he has already served on probation

21. Assume you are a supervisor and an employee must be transferred into your office against his wishes.
    According to this procedure, the box you must sign on the record of transfer is
    A. 6A   B. 8A   C. 6B   D. 8B

22. Under this procedure, in the case of a disability transfer, when must Box 6A on Forms DT414 and DT415 be signed by the personnel officer of the district to which the transfer is being made?
    A. In all cases when either Form DT414 or Form DT415 is used
    B. In all cases when Form DT414 is used and only under certain circumstances when Form DT415 is used
    C. In all cases when Form DT415 is used and only under certain circumstances when Form DT414 is used
    D. Only under certain circumstances when either Form DT414 or Form DT415 is used

23. From the above passage, it may be inferred MOST correctly that the number of copies of Form DT414 is
    A. no more than 2
    B. at least 3
    C. at least 5
    D. more than the number of copies of Form DT415

24. A change in punctuation and capitalization only which would change one sentence into two and possibly contribute to somewhat greater ease of reading this report extract would be MOST appropriate in the
    A. 2nd sentence, 1st paragraph
    B. 3rd sentence, 1st paragraph
    C. next to the last sentence, 2nd paragraph
    D. 2nd sentence, 2nd paragraph

25. In the second paragraph, a word that is INCORRECTLY used is
    A. *shall* in the 1st sentence
    B. *voluntary* in the 3rd sentence
    C. *occurred* in the 4th sentence
    D. *intra-district* in the last sentence

KEY (CORRECT ANSWERS)

1.	C	11.	C
2.	B	12.	B
3.	B	13.	A
4.	B	14.	D
5.	B	15.	B
6.	C	16.	A
7.	D	17.	C
8.	B	18.	B
9.	C	19.	A
10.	D	20.	D

21. D
22. D
23. B
24. B
25. C

INTERPRETING STATISTICAL DATA
GRAPHS, CHARTS AND TABLES
EXAMINATION SECTION
TEST 1

DIRECTIONS: Each questioner incomplete statement is followed by several suggested answers or completions. Select the one that BEST answers the question or completes the statement. *PRINT THE LETTER OF THE CORRECT ANSWER IN THE SPACE AT THE RIGHT.*

Questions 1-3.

DIRECTIONS: Questions 1 through 3 are to be answered SOLELY on the basis of the following table.

QUARTERLY SALES REPORTED BY MAJOR INDUSTRY GROUPS

DECEMBER 2021 – FEBRUARY 2023
Reported Sales, Taxable & Non-Taxable (in Millions)

Industry Groups	12/21-2/22	3/22-5/22	6/22-8/22	9/22-11/22	12/22-2/23
Retailers	2,802	2,711	2,475	2,793	2,974
Wholesalers	2,404	2,237	2,269	2,485	2,974
Manufacturers	3,016	2,888	3,001	3,518	3,293
Services	1,034	1,065	984	1,132	1,092

1. The trend in total reported sales may be described as
    A. downward
    B. downward and upward
    C. horizontal
    D. upward

2. The two industry groups that reveal a similar seasonal pattern for the period December 2021 through November 2022 are
    A. retailers and manufacturers
    B. retailers and wholesalers
    C. wholesalers and manufacturers
    D. wholesalers and service

3. Reported sales were at a MINIMUM between
    A. December 2021 and February 2022
    B. March 2022 and May 2022
    C. June 2022 and August 2022
    D. September 2022 and November 2022

TEST 2

DIRECTIONS: Each question or incomplete statement is followed by several suggested answers or completions. Select the one that BEST answers the question or completes the statement. *PRINT THE LETTER OF THE CORRECT ANSWER IN THE SPACE AT THE RIGHT*

Questions 1-4.

DIRECTIONS: Questions 1 through 4 are to be answered SOLELY on the basis of the following information.

The income elasticity of demand for selected items of consumer demand in the United States are:

Item	Elasticity
Airline Travel	5.66
Alcohol	.62
Dentist Fees	1.00
Electric Utilities	3.00
Gasoline	1.29
Intercity Bus	1.89
Local Bus	1.41
Restaurant Meals	.75

1. The demand for the item listed below that would be MOST adversely affected by a decrease in income is

   A. alcohol
   B. electric utilities
   C. gasoline
   D. restaurant meals

2. The item whose relative change in demand would be the same as the relative change in income would be

   A. dentist fees
   B. gasoline
   C. restaurant meals
   D. none of the above

3. If income increases by 12 percent, the demand for restaurant meals may be expected to increase by

   A. 9 percent
   B. 12 percent
   C. 16 percent
   D. none of the above

4. On the basis of the above information, the item whose demand would be MOST adversely affected by an increase in the sales tax from 7 percent to 8 percent to be passed on to the consumer in the form of higher prices

   A. would be airline travel
   B. would be alcohol
   C. would be gasoline
   D. cannot be determined

TEST 3

DIRECTIONS: Each question or incomplete statement is followed by several suggested answers or completions. Select the one that BEST answers the question or completes the statement. *PRINT THE LETTER OF THE CORRECT ANSWER IN THE SPACE AT THE RIGHT.*

Questions 1-3.

DIRECTIONS: Questions 1 through 3 are to be answered SOLELY on the basis of the following graphs depicting various relationships in a single retail store.

GRAPH 1
RELATIONSHIP BETWEEN NUMBER OF CUSTOMERS STORE AND TIME OF DAY

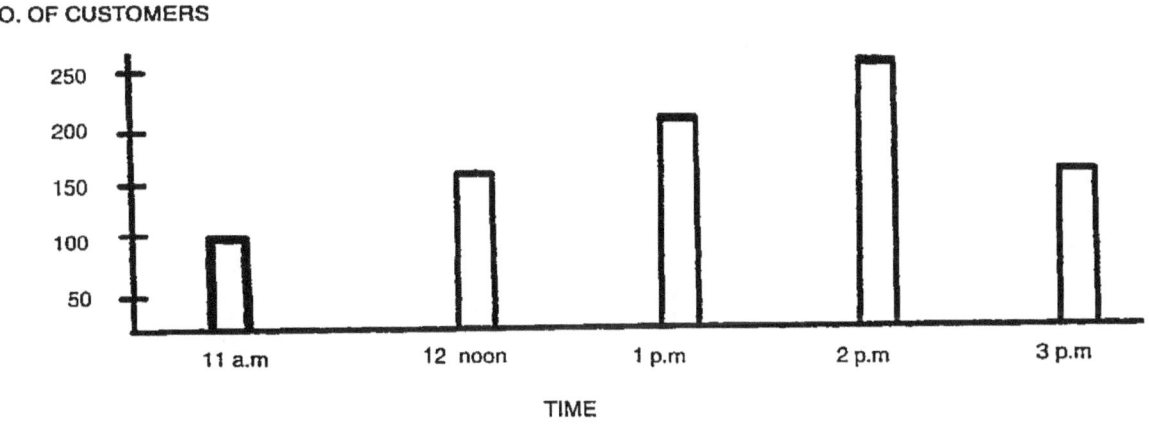

GRAPH II
RELATIONSHIP BETWEEN NUMBER OF CHECK-OUT LANES AVAILABLE IN STORE AND WAIT TIME FOR CHECK-OUT

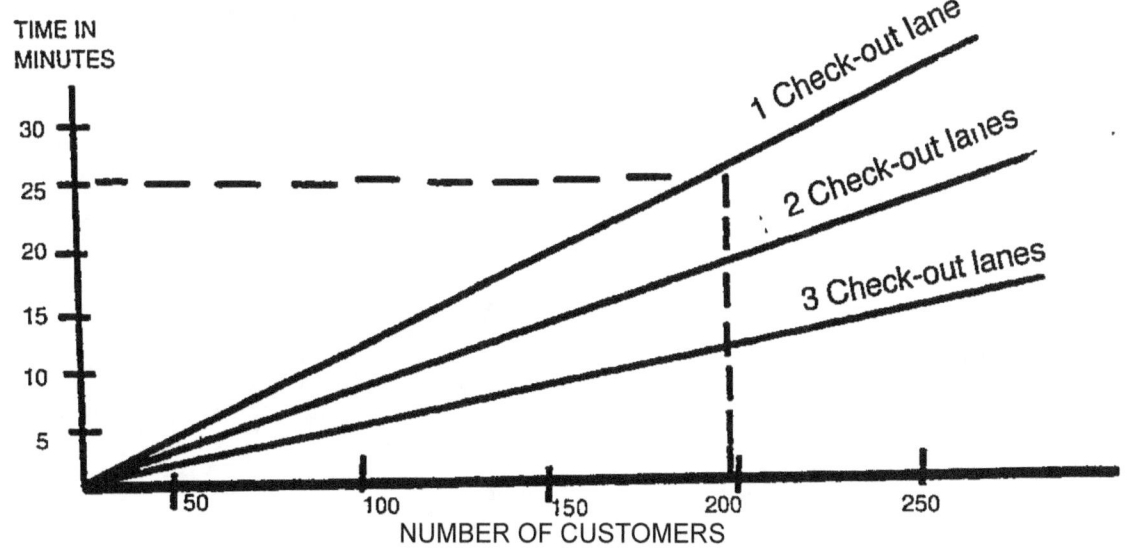

Note the dotted lines in Graph II. They demonstrate that, if there are 200 people in the store and only one check-out lane is open, the wait time will be 25 minutes.

153

1. At what time would a person be most likely NOT to have to wait more than 15 minutes if only one check-out lane is open?

   A. 11 A.M.   B. 12 Noon   C. 1 P.M.   D. 3 P.M.

2. At what time of day would a person have to wait the LONGEST to check out if three check-out lanes are available?

   A. 11 A.M.   B. 12 Noon   C. 1 P.M.   D. 2 P.M

3. The difference in wait times between 1 and 3 check-out lanes at 3 P.M. is MOST NEARLY

   A. 5   B. 10   C. 15   D. 20

TEST 4

DIRECTIONS: Each question or incomplete statement is followed by several suggested answers or completions. Select the one that BEST answers the question or completes the statement. *PRINT THE LETTER OF THE CORRECT ANSWER IN THE SPACE AT THE RIGHT.*

Questions 1-4.

DIRECTIONS: Questions 1 through 4 are to be answered SOLELY on the basis of the graph below.

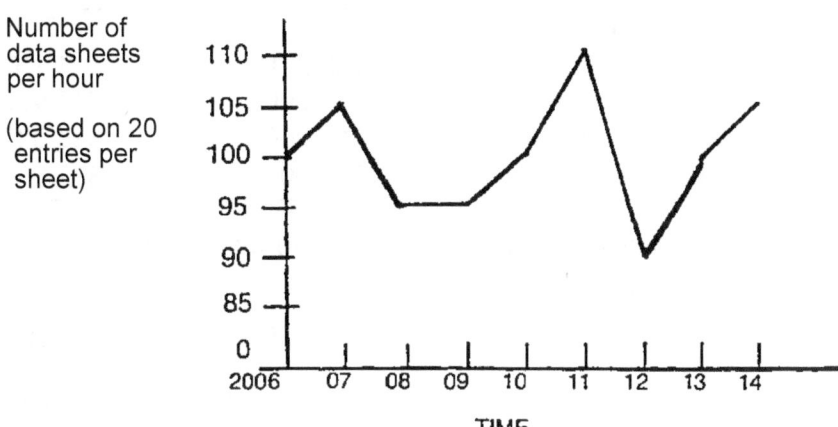

1. Of the following, during what four-year period did the average output of computer operators fall BELOW 100 sheets per hour?

    A. 2007-10   B. 2008-11   C. 2010-13   D. 2011-14

2. The average percentage change in output over the previous year's output for the years 2009 to 2012 is MOST NEARLY

    A. 2   B. 0   C. -5   D. -7

3. The difference between the actual output for 2012 and the projected figure based upon the average increase from 2006-2011 is MOST NEARLY

    A. 18   B. 20   C. 22   D. 24

4. Assume that after constructing the above graph you, an analyst, discovered that the average number of entries per sheet in 2012 was 25 (instead of 20) because of the complex nature of the work performed during that period.
   The average output in sheets per hour for the period 2010-13, expressed in terms of 20 items per sheet, would then be MOST NEARLY

    A. 95   B. 100   C. 105   D. 110

155

TEST 6

DIRECTIONS: Each question or incomplete statement is followed by several suggested answers or completions. Select the one that BEST answers the question or completes the statement. *PRINT THE LETTER OF THE CORRECT ANSWER IN THE SPACE AT THE RIGHT.*

Questions 1-3.

DIRECTIONS: Questions 1 through 3 are to be answered on the basis of the following data assembled for a cost-benefit analysis.

	Cost	Benefit
No program	0	0
Alternative W	$ 3,000	$ 6,000
Alternative X	$10,000	$17,000
Alternative Y	$17,000	$25,000
Alternative Z	$30,000	$32,000

1. From the point of view of selecting the alternative with the best cost benefit ratio, the BEST alternative is Alternative

    A. W   B. X   C. Y   D. Z

2. From the point of view of selecting the alternative with the best measure of net benefit, the BEST alternative is Alternative

    A. W   B. X   C. Y   D. Z

3. From the point of view of pushing public expenditure to the point where marginal benefit equals or exceeds marginal cost, the BEST alternative is Alternative

    A. W   B. X   C. Y   D. Z

TEST 6

DIRECTIONS: Each question or incomplete statement is followed by several suggested answers or completions. Select the one that BEST answers the question or completes the statement. *PRINT THE LETTER OF THE CORRECT ANSWER IN THE SPACE AT THE RIGHT.*

Questions 1-3.

DIRECTIONS: Questions 1 through 3 are to be answered SOLELY on the basis of the following data.

A series of cost-benefit studies of various alternative health programs yields the following results:

Program	Benefit	Cost
K	30	15
L	60	60
M	300	150
N	600	500

In answering Questions 1 and 2, assume that all programs can be increased or decreased in scale without affecting their individual benefit-to-cost ratios.

1. The benefit-to-cost ratio of Program M is

   A. 10:1   B. 5:1   C. 2:1   D. 1:2

2. The budget ceiling for one or more of the programs included in the study is set at 75 units. It may MOST logically be concluded that

   A. Programs K and L should be chosen to fit within the budget ceiling
   B. Program K would be the most desirable one that could be afforded
   C. Program M should be chosen rather than Program K
   D. the choice should be between Programs M and K

3. If no assumptions can be made regarding the effects of change of scale, the MOST logical conclusion, on the basis of the data available, is that

   A. more data are needed for a budget choice of program
   B. Program K is the most preferable because of its low cost and good benefit-to-cost ratio
   C. Program M is the most preferable because of its high benefits and good benefit-to-cost ratio
   D. there is no difference between Programs K and M, and either can be chosen for any purpose

TEST 7

DIRECTIONS: Each question or incomplete statement is followed by several suggested answers or completions. Select the one that BEST answers the question or completes the statement. *PRINT THE LETTER OF THE CORRECT ANSWER IN THE SPACE AT THE RIGHT.*

Questions 1-6.

DIRECTIONS: Questions 1 through 6 are to be answered SOLELY on the basis of the information contained in the charts below which relate to the budget allocations of City X, a small suburban community. The charts depict the annual budget allocations by Department and by expenditures over a five-year period.

CITY X BUDGET IN MILLIONS OF DOLLARS
TABLE I. Budget Allocations by Department

Department	2017	2018	2019	2020	2021
Public Safety	30	45	50	40	50
Health and Welfare	50	75	90	60	70
Engineering	5	8	10	5	8
Human Resources	10	12	20	10	22
Conservation & Environment	10	15	20	20	15
Education & Development	15	25	35	15	15
TOTAL BUDGET	120	180	225	150	180

TABLE II. Budget Allocations by Expenditures

Category	2017	2018	2019	2020	2021
Raw Materials & Machinery	36	63	68	30	98
Capital Outlay	12	27	56	15	18
Personal Services	72	90	101	105	64
TOTAL BUDGET	120	180	225	150	180

1. The year in which the SMALLEST percentage of the total annual budget was allocated to the Department of Education and Development is

   A. 2017   B. 2018   C. 2020   D. 2021

2. Assume that in 2020 the Department of Conservation and Environment divided its annual budget into the three categories of expenditures and in exactly the same proportion as the budget shown in Table II for the year 2020. The amount allocated for capital outlay in the Department of Conservation and Environment's 2020 budget was MOST NEARLY _____ million.

   A. $2   B. $4   C. $6   D. $10

3. From the year 2018 to the year 2020, the sum of the annual budgets for the Departments of Public Safety and Engineering showed an overall _____ million.

   A. decline; $8
   B. increase; $7
   C. decline; $15
   D. increase; $22

4. The LARGEST dollar increase in departmental budget allocations from one year to the next was in _____ from _____.

   A. Public Safety; 2017 to 2018
   B. Health and Welfare; 2017 to 2018
   C. Education and Development; 2019 to 2020
   D. Human Resources; 2019 to 2020

5. During the five-year period, the annual budget of the Department of Human Resources was GREATER than the annual budget for the Department of Conservation and Environment in _____ of the years.

   A. none   B. one   C. two   D. three

6. If the total City X budget increases at the same rate from 2021 to 2022 as it did from 2020 to 2021, the total City X budget for 2022 will be MOST NEARLY _____ million.

   A. $180   B. $200   C. $210   D. $215

TEST 8

DIRECTIONS: Each question or incomplete statement is followed by several suggested answers or completions. Select the one that BEST answers the question or completes the statement. *PRINT THE LETTER OF THE CORRECT ANSWER IN THE SPACE AT THE RIGHT.*

Questions 1-3.

DIRECTIONS: Questions 1 through 3 are to be answered SOLELY on the basis of the following information.

Assume that in order to encourage Program A, the State and Federal governments have agreed to make the following reimbursements for money spent on Program A, provided the unreimbursed balance is paid from City funds.

During Fiscal Year 2021-2022 - For the first $2 million expended, 50% Federal reimbursement and 30% State reimbursement; for the next $3 million, 40% Federal reimbursement and 20% State reimbursement; for the next $5 million, 20% Federal reimbursement and 10% State reimbursement. Above $10 million expended, no Federal or State reimbursement.

During Fiscal Year 2022-2023 - For the first $1 million expended, 30% Federal reimbursement and 20% State reimbursement; for the next $4 million, 15% Federal reimbursement and 10% State reimbursement. Above $5 million expended, no Federal or State reimbursement.

1. Assume that the Program A expenditures are such that the State reimbursement for Fiscal Year 2021-2022 will be $1 million.
   Then, the Federal reimbursement for Fiscal Year 2021-2022 will be

   A. $1,600,000   B. $1,800,000
   C. $2,000,000   D. $2,600,000

2. Assume that $8 million were to be spent on Program A in Fiscal Year 2022-2023.
   The TOTAL amount of unreimbursed City funds required would be

   A. $3,500,000   B. $4,500,000
   C. $5,500,000   D. $6,500,000

3. Assume that the City desires to have a combined total of $6 million spent in Program A during both the Fiscal Year 2021-2022 and the Fiscal Year 2022-2023.
   Of the following expenditure combinations, the one which results in the GREATEST reimbursement of City funds is _____ in Fiscal Year 2021-2022 and _____ in Fiscal Year 2022-2023.

   A. $5 million; $1 million   B. $4 million; $2 million
   C. $3 million; $3 million   D. $2 million; $4 million

KEY (CORRECT ANSWERS)

TEST 1	TEST 2	TEST 3	TEST 4
1. D	1. B	1. A	1. A
2. C	2. A	2. D	2. B
3. C	3. A	3. B	3. C
	4. D		4. C

TEST 5	TEST 6	TEST 7	TEST 8
1. A	1. C	1. D	1. B
2. C	2. D	2. A	2. D
3. C	3. A	3. A	3. A
		4. B	
		5. B	
		6. D	

www.ingramcontent.com/pod-product-compliance
Lightning Source LLC
Chambersburg PA
CBHW081818300426
44116CB00014B/2409